THE DNA OF SUCCESS

THE DNA OF SUCCESS

The Entrepreneurs Guide To
Becoming Deployed, Not Employed.

DONNIE L. NELSON

Dedication

I want to thank my beloved wife Denyelle and my children, Diamond and Elijah Nelson for supporting and encouraging me throughout the writing of this book. You all mean the world to me and I could not have done this without your love and support. I cannot Thank You all enough for allowing me to express and contribute my DNA (Designed Natural Abilities) to the world. I dedicate this book also to those who are in a constant search for a way out of poverty. I was inspired by you to write this book. I know what it feels like to go without eating and having a, I must do whatever it takes to survive mentally. No one gave me a head start in life or any direction. I could be stuck in despair right now, but the discover of my DNA allow me to make it out. My heart's desire is for you also to make out by you discovering your DNA so that it can create a better life for you and your family. Lastly, to the people who are in search of their why. I was moved by the thought of you. A thought that said to me, if I could help a few million people discover their DNA and its contribution to mankind than more jobs will be created. How, because the people who discover who they truly by understanding their DNA become deployed, and those who become deployed become employers that will help to better the lives of countless others. I want to be the first to say Thank You for your contribution to mankind, and I am eternally grateful that you allowed me to be a part of your journey.

Table of Contents Preface

8

FOREWORDS
By Abdul Azim Muhammad

We are in a world where mediocrity rules with an iron fist, clothed in a velvet glove destroying dreams with one insecure thought at a time. A world where the norm is your family and peer circle telling you you're crazy for thinking outside of the box of mediocrity and attempting to become somebody successful. A world that tells you not to wake up in the morning thinking about the sweet-smelling aroma of success but rather the nose consuming stench of fresh average in the morning brewing daily. A world that reinforces mediocrity with special concrete and steel plating to ensure that the majority of people settle for becoming average. Blaming the circumstances of their life on the economy, their job, how they were raised and everyone else but themselves and the choices that they've made. If you no longer want to live in a world that promotes mediocrity, then you must strive to become who your DNA designed you to be. What if I told you that your DNA is designed to get you to a place in life that will ensure a comfortable luxurious ride on your own private jet. How does that sound? I know what you're thinking. I'll have that minus the struggles of life and hard work. However, that is just not possible. Everyman must pay the price because what is given for free is treated like an unwanted stepchild with an uncaring mother. Eventually what was given for free will run away from home or be locked up in someone else's treasure chest if not properly looked after. What is this thing called mastery that comes to mind? Do you think of great athletes, musicians, recording artists and painters? Maybe you think about the 10,000-hours rule popularized by Malcolm Gladwell. That states that anyone who masters anything must spend a grueling 10,000 hours beating away at their craft day by day, year after year until they reach a level of unconscious competence. Maybe you may take it primal where every animal, insect and microscopic being masters its environment and extracts it's wants and needs from the world around them according to their DNA. Maybe you think of the great business minds like the Jay Abraham's, Damon John's, Dan Pena's , Elon Musk's , the JayZ's and Shaun Combs of the world who have mastered their DNA and became successful in the environment they were designed for. There has to come a time in life when a void inside of you thirst to be filled by your unlimited potential. A void that begins to scream so loud that you can no longer ignore it. A voice that tells you that you have a WHY for being on earth. That you were not just born by accident but that you exist on purpose. The fact that you made it from your mother's womb makes you a winner. You won the sperm race. You beat every other spermatozoon (individual sperm cell) to get to your mother's egg. You are a winner born with the DNA that will help you to succeed. I believe by reading this book it will help you to identify your functions which will lead you to finding your DNA, and your DNA will help you to find your meaning in life, so that you can begin to live life on purpose. There is an old saying that states if you search you will find. It's time that you find who you were designed to become. Millions of people spend thousands of hours, days, months and years trying to discover the meaning of life, but they will never discover that meaning without understanding their DNA. The meaning of life resides in who you are and not what you do. If you are anything like me, you have probably asked yourself questions like "Why am I here? Is there something I am meant to do in life? It would be nearly impossible to find someone that exists that has not asked themselves these questions. It is no coincidence that you are sitting down reading this book. To simply put it, you are not reading this book on luck or accident or by chance but on purpose. You are the only person in the world that was designed to become you. You have a purpose in life that only you can complete and the sooner you become who you were designed to be the sooner you will find the success, happiness, and fulfillment you long for. Today your search ends, and your journey begins with discovering the DNA that designed you. Once you begin to discover your innate abilities and the DNA that you were born with, you start to become successful. The sole purpose of this book is to help you locate your success by helping you discover your DNA. Your DNA is not hard to find you are not as complicated as you may think. Many others have exhausted the possibilities of these questions through the annals of time and have left the blueprints to unlock the secrets of your design encoded in your DNA. It's time that you discover the answers to what your DNA designed you to become. The inherent abilities and functions that your DNA placed within you are unique. No one has the DNA to become you. The DNA placed within you is the very things that make you who you are. Now is the time to crack the code to your potential and spread your wings and fly beyond the expectations of others and even your own imagination. All you have to do is be willing to experience a revelation, the revelation of your true self. Seek, and you will find, knock, and the door will open. You would not be reading this book if you were not in search of success, so I'm grateful you are taking the steps into finding your uniqueness. I compel you to read this book to the end and then sign up for a free coaching session. The greatest trial in life is not death, it's never obtaining a revelation of what your DNA designed you to be. Before you take this voyage into this terra incognita (uncharted territory) I leave you with the words of T. E. Lawrence. "All men dream but not equally. Those who dream by night in the dusty recesses of their minds wake in the day to find that it was vanity, but the dreamers of the day are dangerous men for they may act on their dreams with open eyes to make them possible. ". So, dream with your eyes and mind open to new possibilities and experiences. This is the beginning of a new life for you, a life where you are deployed and not employed.

Chapter 1

Success Is In Your DNA

"DNA is like a computer program but far, far more advanced than any software ever created."
— *Bill Gates*

"I want to change history, do something important in my life, and influence individuals like we have with millions of small businesses. "Then they love and respect you because you made their life important."

Jack Ma, the founder and former CEO of Alibaba. Alibaba and Jack Ma, may not be household names outside of China, but Alibaba is worth more than Facebook, and processes more goods and orders than eBay and Amazon combined, making Ma the richest man in China with an estimated net worth of $25 billion at the time of this writing. Today, Ma is considered one of the most successful individuals of our time but that was not always the case. Born as Ma Yun in Hangzhou, during the rise of the communist rule in china. As a young boy Ma became interested in learning the English Language. He was giving the opportunity to learn English after former President Richard Nixon visited Hangzhou in 1972. This visit by a President improved the situation of tourism allowing Hangzhou to become a popular tourist destination. This provided Ma with the opportunity to became a tour guide to foreign tourist in exchange for English lessons. This is also where he met and befriended a foreign girl who gave him the nickname Jack. Although, very success driven Ma's teenage years where no reflections of that. He was met with much failure and that continued on into his adulthood. Failing the entrance exam for the Hangzhou Teachers College twice. He was finally admitted on the third try, in 1984.

While trying to earn his bachelor's degree Ma tried and failed to get several jobs he applied for. Ma states in an interview with 60 Minutes that when KFC came to China. That twenty-four people went for the job and twenty-three people were accepted. He was the only one that did not get accepted. He also recounted the time that him and four people went to apply for a job on the police force and he was the only one that got rejected after being told, "No, you're no good." Finally graduating with a bachelor's degree in English in 1988 he went on to teach English at the Hangzhou Institute of Electronics and Engineering (now Hangzhou Dianzi University), for a pay of $12 a month until 1993. In 1994, he founded his first company, the Haibo Translation Agency, which provided English translation and interpretation. Ma went on to fail in this venture and a few others, but that didn't stop him in any way of dreaming bigger. In 1995, Ma took a trip to the United States on behalf of the Hangzhou City government to complete a project related to building highways. It was on that trip that he was introduced to computers and the internet. At this time computers were non-existent in China given the high costs associated with them. During Ma's stay in the U.S he was given the opportunity to try out a computer. His first search on the internet (the mosaic browser) was beer and it returned results from different countries, but signs of China were nowhere. He then searched 'China' and not a single result was found. It was at that moment he decided it was time for China and its people to get on the Internet.

This was the turning point of Ma's life. He went back to China and founded China Pages, which created Websites for Chinese businesses and was one of China's first Internet companies. He left the company two years later, however, partly because of strong competition from the communications company Hangzhou Telecom, which founded a rival company, Chinese pages. From 1998 to 1999, Ma was head of an Internet company in Beijing that was backed by the Ministry of Foreign Trade and Economic Cooperation. One day he felt that if he remained with the government, he would miss out on the economic opportunities that the Internet was bringing. So, Ma went to work the next day and persuaded 17 of his friends and team members at the ministry to go back to Hangzhou with him and they Co-founded the Alibaba Group, which launched a Website that facilitated deals between small businesses. Ma was convinced that the small-business-to-small-business internet market had much greater potential for growth than the business-to-consumer internet market had. So, after persuading 17 of his other friends to invest and join him in his new e-commerce startup. Alibaba, the company began from his apartment not having a single penny in investment from outside investors, but they later raised $20 Million from Softbank and another $5 Million from Goldman Sachs in 1999.

Finally, Ma started his first successful company at the age of 31. What's more amazing is he did all of this without having to write a single line of code or selling anything to anyone. The company went on to grow rapidly, expanding all across the world, quickly growing out of its China shell. In 2005 Alibaba attracted the attention of the American Internet portal Yahoo!, which bought a 40 percent stake, and in 2007 Alibaba.com raised $1.7 billion dollars in its initial public offering (IPO) in Hong Kong. The ripped growth of Alibaba continued into September 2014 when the Alibaba Group debuted an IPO on the New York Stock Exchange that raised $21.8 billion.

That IPO was the largest ever in the United States and gave the company a market value of $168 billion, the highest such value in IPO history at that time for an Internet company. Alibaba became the E-commerce giant that Jack Ma had envisioned for it. Just like Jack Ma, every human on earth wants to be successful! He could have given up, caved in and, quit many times but he didn't and that's why we have Alibaba today. The desire to succeed is inherent in human nature and is a primary drive for all human decisions and actions. It's why some people scheme, compete, and war with each other. It's why we establish relationships with significant people, and networks. It's also why we get an education, start businesses or look for promotions within the job we chose. We want success. Anyone who says they do not want to succeed in life, we should be concerned about. Even the guy sleeping under the bridge desires success. Anyone who claims they do not desire to be successful is being totally dishonest.

The desire for success feeds the human need for purpose, passion and pursuit. It gives the human spirit the motivation to dream. The desire for success is an individual's reason for progress, development and refinement. Some may define success in our materialistic world as fame and popularity. Success may result from these things, but they are not the definition of success.

I believe the best way to define success is by taking a look at those who you may consider successful. You may consider Steve Jobs, Nelson Mandela, Jack Ma, Martin Luther King Jr., Elon Musk, Abraham Lincoln, Michael Jordan, Sarah Blakey, Nikola Tesla, Mahatma Gandhi, Walt Disney, Larry Page, Sergey Brin, Albert Einstein, and Kevin Plank. If you were to analyze any of these individuals, it will reveal that success was not a product of their intelligence, education, social status, upbringing or even where they came from, but the success of each was related to the discovery, understanding, development, and contribution of their Designed Natural Abilities (DNA). Not one of these individuals pursued success, but rather they were all in pursuit of their inherent design and the contributions that it would bring to their generation. As a result of this they became successful. Success, therefore, has very little to do with being famous, popular, recognized, or having lots of money, but rather it is the result of one's DNA.

You would not know Tiger Woods if he decided to pursue basketball rather than golf. You would not know Jay Z if he decided to pursue being a drug kingpin rather than rapper. You would not know former President Barack

Obama if he decided to pursue medicine rather than public service. You would not know Winston Churchill if he decided to pursue business rather than Servant leadership. We know them because they decided to follow their DNA.

When you discover and present your DNA to the world you become valuable to humanity and people who become valuable are described as "successful". In essence, success is about discovery. Discovering the value of your DNA and sharing it contribution. That is what this book is about, because every human on earth came with an inherent set of DNA. Every living and created thing on earth was manufactured with success. Take a moment and look around. Everything, you see is designed to succeed. From the devices you see around you to the chair you are setting in. There is not a created thing that cannot produce its own success. For example, every seed has within it a plant and the success of that seed is the plant. In Other words, the moment that a seed becomes a tree/flower it has produced and discovered success. When you become what your DNA manufactured you to be you'll find success. The DNA you carry is a natural resource it's unique, significant, rare and valuable. Your success is not outside of you, it's in you. If you genuinely want to become successful, you have to become the person your DNA designed you to be because your value will be found there. Success will always be located in your value because value equal worth and worth equals wealth. Success is attracted to value. So, if you want to become successful don't seek success, don't seek to become great, don't seek to become influential, and don't seek to become rich and powerful only seek to become valuable by becoming who your DNA designed you to be. When you become valuable wealth, influence, power, and success will find its way to you.

27

Your make-up is designed to bring you opportunities and to put you in the presence of powerful people. It's meant to make you stand out from the rest. My DNA has led me, a little boy eating out of government boxes just to survive to shaking hands with billionaires. Where your DNA will take you, I don't know, but I do know that somewhere will be in the presence of great people who will take your life to the next level. When you discover, refine and serve the design of your DNA success will follow.

When you are valuable success finds you.

Diamonds don't look for people, people look for diamonds because Diamonds are valuable. Metal does not search for people; people search for metal because metal is valuable. Oil doesn't go digging for people; people go digging for oil because oil is valuable. Think about all the things oil is needed for. Oil fuels the cars, trucks, and planes that support and help drive economies and lifestyles. By products of oil consist of plastics, lubricants, tars, asphalts, and pesticides. I think it would be safe to assume that you see the value in oil.

When you discover the reason people need you, you discover your DNA and its contribution. You are worth what you are valued. You will find this to be very factual when you enter the economy. The more value that you bring to the economy the more the economy will pay. The less valuable you are to the economy the less the economy will pay. The economy pays you what you are valued. If someone helps others to become better or can help a company, make billions. Would you not agree that the economy should pay that person millions? Would not that person be worth it? Would not that person be needed? It's probably safe to say that person is valuable. What about the person that makes 10 dollars an hour? It would be safe to say that, that person is not that valuable to his economy. They may be valuable to their friends and to their family but not to the economy. You will always be paid for your value. People pay for gold because of its value, and people will pay for you because of your value.

You cannot become successful without discovering how your DNA designed you. It's the only thing that can define your purpose. I describe The Design Of DNA as (The complete make-up of a thing that has the inherent capacity to fulfill an intended purpose). When you took a moment to look at the things around you I am willing to bet that there is not one single thing that you laid eyes on that did not have an intended purpose for use. Everything in creation is designed with the ability to fulfill an intended purpose, from the things that are man-made to man itself. The more aware you become of how

30

your DNA designed you the easier it will be for you to discover your purpose and contribution to mankind.

The way you are assembled, your abilities, the things that you are capable of doing, to the potential you hold, it was all constructed for an intended purpose. You are not an accident, you're not a biological mistake. You are here to fulfill an intended purpose. You were distinctly chosen by the universe because of your DNA. Your DNA host abilities that are needed to help all of creation with a specific problem. You are the answer to someone's problem and when you are the answer you begin to discover value, and value creates wealth.

It's already in you.

Whatever your DNA designed you to become the ability to become it exists within you. The DNA of all things is hidden within its design.

For instance, if you were to analyze the design and life of Rhianna and how she sang with such amazement. You will discover that she came from a poverty stricken and abusive environment let alone being able to afford singing lessons. So, without a single lesson on singing and very little education she became a superstar. The ability to sing already existed within her. Singing is not something she learned to do but, who she already was. Your DNA, invents, creates and fashions the success you desire to see. It's responsible for the successes or failures you see in life. Vera Wang found out how true this was on her journey to success.

She began her journey as a professional figure skater but failed to make the U.S. Olympic figure-skating team at the age of 19. This helps her to realize that being a professional skater was not something she was designed to become. She then turned her attention to fashion and got a job at Yves Saint Laurent boutique on New York's Madison Avenue. This led her to meet Frances Patiky Stein while shopping at Saint Laurent. Frances was one of the two fashion directors of American Vogue at the time. Frances said to the young Vera call me when you're finished with college. Two years later she called and got a job as a temporary assistant at American Vogue. She quickly worked her way up the ladder becoming one of the magazines youngest ever fashion editors.

When you discover the design of your DNA, the universe will conspire to bring out the potential that exists within you to transform you into what your DNA designed you to become. So, Vera spent the next 15 years at the magazine becoming and developing her potential until she was passed over for the editor-in-chief position and decided it was time to leave to become more. She was 38 years old. She ended up taking a job at Ralph Lauren as a design director. When you become aware of the potential that exists within your DNA nothing can stop you from trying to find out what you can become. Your potential pushes you to new boundaries. That's exactly what it did for Vera, and two years later Vera Wang became a designer, and her empire is worth more than $1billion today.

Your design and what you were built to become is a part of learning who you truly are. You must be on a constant hunt to find out how your DNA manufactured you. If you are not than, a perpetual state of failure will become inevitable in your life. You cannot ignore that fact that you were created a certain way, because doing so will cause you to become confused, and issues of personal identity will become a challenge and success becomes a struggle. As a matter of fact, from the time, we are very young we begin to test different versions of our DNA at different points in life. We try to imitate the things that appeal to us the most. We do this because we don't have confidence in our own DNA. We have no idea about who we are or what we can become. Therefore, we begin to be influenced by the people around us, not knowing that these people are struggling with their own identity. You will never become successful being a cheap copy of someone else. A bird's DNA designed it to fly, so you will never find it trying to swim. You were not designed to become the individual/s who exert influence over you; rather it's a friend, parent, teacher, coach or celebrity. The key is to learn from those influences not to become them.

Chapter 2

The Destination Of DNA

The bottom line is: We must be working on arriving at the destination for which we were put on this planet

-Yehuda Berg

When I think about people who have literally climbed their way to success from the very bottom to get to the destination in which their DNA designed them for, Shawn Carter comes to mind. Born in 1969, in the projects of Brooklyn, the man we now know today as Jay Z. Raised by a single mother with his three older siblings after being abandoned by their father. Growing up in a crime and drug infested neighborhood Jay Z dropped out of high school, to sell crack cocaine to make money for him and his family. Jay Z was able to turn some of this depravity into art. He did so by turning to rap at a young age as an escape from the drugs, violence and poverty that surrounded him in the Marcy Projects. In 1989, he joined the rapper Jaz-O an older performer who served as a kind of mentor to record a song called "The Originators," which won the pair an appearance on an episode of *Yo! MTV Raps*. It was at this point that Carter embraced the nickname Jay-Z, which was simultaneously an homage to Jaz-O, and a reference to the J/Z subway station near his Brooklyn home. As an incredibly talented lyricist, he would compete and win freestyle competitions all around his city, making a reputation for himself. It has been stated that he read the dictionary cover to cover on multiple occasions, giving him a better vocabulary to rhyme. When you understand the place, your DNA has you going then the road that leads you there becomes easy to find. This is what pushed Jay to keep going with little to no success securing a record deal. Every major label in the country turned him down. Rather than let that get him down and turn him back to his old life and all the crime, Jay Z decided to take another route to get to his destination. He became a producer himself and started his own label with two friends, Damon Dash and Kareem Burke, called Roc-a-Fella Records, in 1996. In June of that year, Jay-Z released his debut album, *Reasonable Doubt*. Although the record only reached No. 23 on the *Billboard* 200, it is now considered a classic hip-hop album, including songs such as "Can't Knock the Hustle," featuring <u>Mary J. Blige</u>, and "Brooklyn's Finest," a collaboration with Notorious B.I.G. *Reasonable Doubt* established Jay-Z as an emerging star in hip-hop. The following year, in 1998, Jay Z released *Vol. 2* and the song "Hard Knock Life" and, well, the rest is history. Roc-A-Fella shot up and became quite successful and was later sold to Def Jam Records for millions of dollars. As for Jay Z, he became the President and CEO and took the whole merged label by storm. As president of Def Jam, Jay-Z signed such popular acts as Rihanna and Ne-Yo, and helped West's transition from producer to a best-selling recording artist. But his reign at the venerable hip-hop label wasn't all smooth sailing; Jay-Z resigned as Def Jam's president in 2007, complaining about the company's resistance to change from ineffectual business models. It has been said that he stated to the managers of the label "You have record executives who've been sitting in their office for 20 years because of one act." Staying on the destination in which he was designed for Jay signed a $150 million contract with the concert promotion company Live Nation in 2008. This super deal created a joint venture called Roc Nation, an entertainment company that handles nearly all aspects of its artists' careers. Along with Jay-Z, Roc Nation signed such top artists as Rihanna, Shakira and T.I., among many others, to its roster. Jay-Z's other business ventures include the popular urban clothing line RocaWear and Roc-a-Fella Films. He also owns the 40/40 Club, an upscale sports bar that opened in New York City and later added venues in Atlantic City NJ and Atlanta GA. A part-owner of the New Jersey Nets basketball team a full-service sports management company, called Roc Nation Sports, and a music streaming service called Tidal in which he sold a 33% stake to *telecommunications giant Sprint. In June 2019, Forbes* named Jay-Z the first billionaire rap artist, citing his ownership stakes in Armand de Brignac champagne and Uber as contributing factors.

Travel the road of your DNA.

Just like Jay your success will only be found traveling the road of your DNA. If your

DNA designed you to act and all your innate abilities points you in that direction but instead you become an accountant. Your life will always feel void and meaningless because you're doing something your DNA never designed you to do although you may be good at it.

You will never find success in doing something that does not line-up with your DNA.

I had a few friends who loved 4-wheeling. One day we all went out to do just that, and another mutual friend of ours came along who had just bought a 2-wheel drive Jeep. We had fun for hours on this incredible dirt trail. My friend with the 2-wheel drive was doing surprisingly well, but the dirt began to get a little muddy, and he eventually got stuck and could not get out because his vehicle did not have a 4-wheel drive function like the other vehicles. A 2-wheel drive vehicle was never designed to do 4-

wheeling on muddy dirt roads because it lacked the functions necessary to get the job done. So many people look for jobs and take careers that their DNA never designed them for. They do things and take part in things that don't fit their DNA. Time after time we try to fit a square in a circle when it never fits. I'm a speaker and for me to try to travel down a path as a singer would be for me to commit success suicide.

Do things that will cause you to be yourself.

When you do something your DNA never designed you to do, you are not yourself, and when you are not being yourself life no longer becomes enjoyable but a complete struggle. The feeling of doing something your DNA designed you for, fulfills your heart desires and life purpose. There is no greater feeling than doing something that allows you, to be you. When you are doing something that permits you to be you, people have to tell you to stop working because you never get tired of being yourself. That's why it's essential to follow the DNA you were designed with.

If you allow it, your DNA will lead you down the road to becoming yourself. When you travel down a road that was never designed for you, it forces you to separate yourself from your inherent nature. You will never become you, being something, your DNA did not design. Acting outside of who you are, will design a person you will become disappointed in. I have found that people who complain the most about their jobs and their lives are those who are living a life not a part of their DNA. Sometimes we get confused because we become good at something and we think that it must be a fit. If you do something long enough you eventually become good at it, but would you do what you are doing

44

without getting paid or recognized? Would you do it as a hobby? Would you do it to the point people have to tell you to stop? Does it feel the purpose void in your life? Does it continuously feel like work? If you could stop and do something else, would you? If you answered honestly to most of those questions than what you are good at is not what your DNA designed you for. If your DNA designed you to do it, then the answers to the above questions will either confirm that you are operating within the design of your DNA or you are allowing life to mode you into something you are not.

Follow your DNA.

When you do something that connects you to your DNA, you will find fulfillment, happiness, and opportunities. To follow your DNA is to follow your nature and when you follow your nature, it will lead you to the

Highway to Success and the Highway to Success will take you to your destination (your life's purpose). So, I compel you to start traveling down the road of your DNA, so that it helps you to locate The Highway to Success. If your DNA designed you to game, then travel that road. If your DNA designed you to make music, then travel that road. Don't take a job that takes you down a different road. Find a job that takes you down the road your DNA designed you to travel until you are able to make a living from what your DNA designed you to do. If your DNA designed you to teach, do not take a job as a telemarketer found a job that will allow you to use the abilities you were born with.

Your destination is in your DNA, not in the opinions of what people want you to become. You are the way you are because your DNA demands you to be that way, so follow your DNA. People are going to criticize and judge you when you don't conform to their ideology about what and how you should be. If your DNA designed you to travel a certain road, then travel it no matter what people think. Follow your DNA and success will follow you on the path you were called to travel. I must warn you that when you enter Success Highway things get a little tough because life has a unique way of testing you. Traveling down Success Highway will cause many distractions along the way because there are no bad exits on a highway. So, if you happen to take a wrong one, it won't be because you thought it was wrong, but because you thought it was right. This is how distractions find their way into your life. Distractions will never appear to be bad. Distractions will always appear to be right otherwise how could it distract you. I find this to be the number one success killer. I have watched distractions kill dreams, visions, and purpose.

So, don't let a distraction seduce you into leaving Success Highway to travel down a road that will inevitably lead you to a destination that does not line up with your DNA. A destination that will eventually lead to an unhappy and unfulfilling life. Anything that pulls you away from operating in the design of your DNA is a distraction. Money can become a distraction. People can become a distraction especially the ones whom never seem like a distraction. A job can be a distraction because they can pay you more money to keep you operating in something that you were not designed to do. Problems can become a distraction because they can take your focus away from doing what your DNA designed you for. Opportunities can become distractions because they offer benefits that cause you to abandon your DNA. All distractions are good if they were bad than they could not distract you. What is distracting you from operating in your DNA? Is it people? Is it money? Is it an opportunity? Is it a problem? What is it? You will never reach your destination being distracted by exits that have nothing to do with your DNA. Your DNA is the ultimate thing that will lead you to success.

The way your DNA designed you and how you were made to function will be inseparable to your success in life. If your DNA designed you to sing, then music is a part of your success and you cannot have one without the other.

If your DNA designed you to inspire people, then being a leader will become a part of your success and the two are inseparable. Your DNA helps you to fulfill your success. The way you function and how you are designed are the key components to achieving success. Your success will never be outside of your functions. Your functions determine the way your DNA designed you so that you can reach success.

That's why you just can't take any exit on Success Highway. It has to be the exit that fits your function and design.

Chapter 3

The Passion In Your DNA

It is obvious that we can no more explain a passion to a person who has never experienced it than we can explain light to the blind."

– T.S. Elliot

The success of every product is built into its DNA. Knowing what activates the contents of that DNA is what will trigger its reason to make an impact, and contribution to our world. I remember learning about a Junior School teacher who got so inspired by the one thing that triggered her DNA that she quit her job as a public-school teacher to become a missionary school teacher for the poor. She decided to take on this challenge in one of the poorest cities in our world today, Calcutta, which is now known as Kolkata the capital of the Indian state of West Bengal. Whenever she went to school she walked through a place that you and I would probably call hell on earth. The path she traveled every day was filled with diseases and people laying in the mud with flies repetitively attaching themselves to their bodies. She stepped over dead bodies that died during the night. She wept every day she traveled to class until one day she became so angry that she brought action to the situation. She became convicted by the things she was experiencing.

Find your conviction.

The conviction within her stirred up hatred in her heart, and that hatred turned into anger. Something has to make you angry. Until you are angry, you have not discovered the very heart of your DNA. What you are built to change triggers a strong emotional feeling in your being, and It's that emotion that connects you to the heart of your DNA and purpose. That is why we call it passion.

Passion moves you to anger because it makes you aware of what you are built to change, and what you are built to change pushes you to act. The teacher quit her job to go and care for the poor. While resigning from her job her supervisor expressed his thoughts to her about quitting and tried to talk her out of it, but there was no way that he could. She asked for her last paycheck and took off. That same day she went to the market spent her entire check on fruits and veggies to feed the people on the open streets. That was the day Mother Teresa was born.

Usually, when people are sad, they don't do anything. They just cry over their condition. But when they get angry, they bring about a change." - Malcolm X

Mother Teresa was not the only person to travel that road every day, but she was the only one who recognized the things that triggered her DNA and allowed it to become a conviction. When you have an uneasiness and restlessness in your heart for something you believe you have a conviction, and a conviction is necessary on your journey to becoming who you were designed to be. It moves you toward an emotion that resembles anger. It's an intense feeling that speaks to you until you begin to move toward an action that satisfies its purpose. Martin Luther King Jr. acted on his conviction. Gandhi acted on his conviction. Rosa Parks acted on her conviction. Abraham Lincoln acted on this conviction. They would not have affected the world if they had not acted on their conviction. A conviction is the only kind of belief that will move you to sacrifice your life to fulfill the purpose of your DNA. When you are willing to die to discover who you are nothing will prevent you from becoming it.

Martin Luther King Jr, Gandhi, Rosa park, Winston Churchill, Nelson Mandela, and Abraham Lincoln were all willing to die for what they believed they had to become to contribute to their generation. What is your conviction about who you are to become to contribute to your generation?

Passion does not allow you to become average.

Operating in your DNA will cause people to call you reckless and crazy because it will never allow you to do things at a moderate level. I can just imagine all the bad press Mother Teresa got on her journey to making a difference in the lives of the poverty-stricken people of Calcutta. I know many people told her that it would be foolish and a big waste of her time to help change the reality of poverty-stricken people. However, when you discover what you are to become your mind cannot turn itself off or down. It drives you to live with an intent to make an impact, that will bring about changes. It fuels our motivation, inspires us to create opportunities for a better destiny (for us or for those whom we care for). It's what defines our entity.

It's what inspired Wendy Kopp to found Teach For America. A diverse network of leaders who confront the educational inequity through teaching and work with an unwavering commitment from every sector of society to create a nation free from injustice. While going for a Bachelor of Art at Princeton University, she discovered that there was a severe disparity in the educational system in the United States. She became so connected to this discovery that she decided to make this her thesis. While doing research and writing her thesis she found that there was a shortage of teachers and a push to get college graduates on Wall Street, but no push to fix the crippling effect of the inequity and injustice in her country's educational system. She recognized that if she did not play a part in changing the realm of inequity in the education system that it would continue to drive the poverty, racism, crime and other rooted injustices that came from a lack of a proper education. So, the triggering of her DNA motivated her to do something to change the injustice in the educational system. She has been quoted saying that when the idea came to her head that she could change a country's problem, she obsessed about it day and night, that her thesis became her blueprint for her plan to change the inequality of the educational system. So, in 1989 in her own words in an interview with National Public Radio, she stated.

"Well, in the last week of writing the thesis, I decided, I'm just going to say to my professor in the thesis that I'm going to go do this. So, he liked the idea, but he thought it was really crazy to think that I was really going to try to go do this. So, I had this plan, and one of the things I had looked at was the origin of the Peace Corps. There's this incredible paper, and in that paper, was this beautiful analysis that concluded that it had to start with 500 core members, that was the smallest possible number that would seem nationally important, but that it was a workable number. Anything bigger would be unmanageable. So that became my number. Like, OK, we've got to recruit 500 people.

Your true Passion is found when you are so moved emotionally by the problems your DNA was designed to solve in the lives of others.

The whole plan was to inspire thousands of people to apply in the first year, and select, and train and place no fewer than 500 of them in, you know, five or six communities across the country. And I had a budget saying, this was going to cost $2.5 million in the first year. And my thesis advisor became really obsessed with that number. Like, how are you going to raise $2.5 million? And he said, you know, do you know how hard it is to raise $2,500? And he sat me down.

He said, I'll tell you what. I'm going to link you up with the head of development at Princeton who's going to explain how hard it is to raise $2,500. When you are moved by your design, the word impossible doesn't register in your heart or mind. Impossible is something that never comes to your mind. People who recognize their DNA intend to do things that are impossible. Even though her professor called her deranged by thinking that she could do the impossible. Wendy left his office and did the impossible. She raised 2.5 million dollars and recruited and trained 489 college graduates without having any training or teaching experience. When a person discovers his or her DNA it will lead them to impact a country. Knowing the design of your DNA will give you an internal drive that will keep you going no matter what. That's why the only people who can keep going after being knocked down are the ones who become conscious of their DNA.

In 1993, a young woman became Jobless, divorced, and penniless with a dependent child. She had no other way to provide for her child, and so she went on government-assisted welfare. While constantly being knocked down by life she never allowed it to stop her from operating in her DNA. Two years later she finished her book manuscript. She sent it out to 12 different major publishers, and they all rejected her book. But because of her staying committed to her DNA, she persisted, and a year later, a small publisher gave her a small advance of £1500 and published just 1000 copies of her book. Today, J.K Rowling has sold more than 400 million copies of her Harry Potter books and is worth more than $1 billion today.

Les Brown stated that

"Wanting something is not enough. You must hunger for it. Your motivation must be absolutely compelling in order to overcome the obstacles that will invariably come your way."

Your DNA is the only thing that can make you believe that you can change the world. It's the thing that lets you know you are living to make a difference. I remember watching a movie a while back called The Family That Preys. One of the characters in the movie by the name of Charlotte stated to Alice "Are you living or are you existing". Deep down inside of every human is a desire not just to exist but to make a contribution with the life they were given. If you just go with the flow of life, follow trends, chase the crowd and live reactively to your environment than you are just existing. The only way for you to live is to do something that connects you to your DNA. Instead, I watch people lock who they are, what they love and want to do in a box to pretend to be something they are not to be accepted. I also watch people work at jobs they hate, do things they don't like, buy stuff they don't want and hang out with people they don't really like just to fit in. You were never designed to fit in but to stand out.

Bill Gates was so aware of his DNA and connection it had to software that he created Microsoft. Before Microsoft Bill was an inexperienced computer programmer who understood the connection between his DNA and writing computer code. That connection was so strong that in the eighth grade, he constantly managed to get excused from math class to design things like the first early video games. When you are operating in your DNA you will notice that the below action will become a part of your life.

How to recognize when you are connected to your DNA.

You will begin to sleep less because your DNA will have you so excited about what you are doing that you will go to bed late thinking about the thing that stimulates your DNA, and that same excitement will get you out of bed early.

You will find you are connected to your DNA when you become obsessed.

When you are operating in your DNA you will not be able to keep your mind from continuously thinking about it because of the excitement that it brings to your heart. When people are enlightened about their DNA it traps them in a world of their own, and this causes them to bind the world to what they believe. Mostly all charismatic and magnetic types of people live by their DNA.

You will find that your DNA is connected to the things that make you angry.

You are extremely emotionally connected to the thing/s your DNA is designed to fix. My wife's DNA for beauty, style, and make-up causes her to cringe and become angry when she sees an actor or host on television and their style, make-up or hair is done in an incorrect way. It gets her so twisted on the inside, and she doesn't ever recognize it.

You will find that your DNA will cause you to risk it all.

People who follow their DNA go all out for the thing/s they believe they are designed for. That's why they are willing to gamble their whole life savings and everything they have to fulfill the design of their DNA.

You will find you are connected to your DNA when you never stop working.

DNA is not just some made up thing it's defines who you are and what you are, so for you to stop following your DNA would be for you to stop being yourself. When you are operating in your DNA, you never work because doing what you love is a part of your nature and that's what makes you, **You**. You'll never work being yourself.

You will find you are connected to your DNA when you can't stop talking about it.

Everyone hates talking to you because they know once they get you going the thing your DNA designed you for will not stop pouring out of your mouth. This is because when you are enlightened about what your DNA designed you for what else is there to talk about.

You will find you are operating in your DNA because you stop living in the present.

People who understand their DNA are so far ahead in their minds that the present is just a moment in time and the future is where they live. Next is always on their mind. The more consciously aware you become of your DNA, you will find characteristic traits in you that you didn't know existed, but those traits are there because they reflect the design of your DNA.

Understanding your DNA will begin to create a new being, a new person, someone you have not seen before. Mother Teresa's DNA designed her to change the condition of the poor in her community, and it compelled her to become someone she never saw before.

J.K Rowling's DNA designed her to tell stories, and it compelled her to become someone she never saw before.

Wendy Kopp's DNA designed her to fight inequality and it compelled her to become someone she never saw before.

What has your DNA designed you for? When you discover it, it will compel you to become someone you never saw.

Chapter 4

The Functions Inside Your DNA

If you get the inside right, the outside will fall into place. Primary reality is within; secondary reality without."

— *Eckhart Toll*

Do you remember when you learned how to walk? The answer is probably no because it was inherent. Whatever it may be, everyone inherently has a function that gives them the ability to do something. Those abilities could be athletic, mathematical, intellectual, artistic, or creative you may have the function to sing, act, dance, public speak, teach, talk, entertain, engineer, or innovate, but because it has become such a part of who you are, you don't recognize the function/ability. What you are designed to become is determined by how your DNA created you to function. The more aware you become of these functions the more these functions begin to reveal your potential. They makes-up everything you are. They provide you with the necessary abilities to fulfill your given purpose.

Fulfilling your function.

When you were created, you were designed in a way that would allow you to fulfill your functions. That's why you have certain qualities and characteristics. You were designed to complete the purpose you were intended for. The way you are and the abilities you possess are inherent, they existed within you before birth.

For example, a person decided one day that they no longer wanted to sit around waiting for a stove oven to cook or reheat their food, so they decided to create a device that could cook or reheat food in minutes. Before the machine had the ability to fulfill the above purpose, the manufacturer had to decide how it would heat and cook the food. Deciding how it would do this becomes the function of the machine and that function determine its design. Built into every microwave is a microwave generator called a magnetron. The magnetron takes electricity from the power outlet and converts it into high powered radio waves. The magnetron then blasts these waves into the food compartment through a channel called a wave guide (this is its function) It's design then allows the microwaves to bounce back and forth off the reflective metal walls of the food compartment, just like light bounces off a mirror. When the microwaves reach the food, they don't simply bounce off but instead the microwaves penetrate inside the food. As they travel through it they make the molecules inside it vibrate more quickly. Vibrating molecules have heat so the faster the molecules vibrate the hotter the food becomes. Thus, the microwaves pass their energy onto the molecules in the food rapidly heating it up.

These are the functions needed for the machine to fulfill its purpose. Therefore, without these functions, the microwave would not be able to carry out its reason for existing. Your DNA created and designed you in a way that would allow you to fulfill your functions. Your outgoing personality, your gift of gab, your ability to sing, your creative mind, your ability to produce magic with your hands, your effortlessness to communicate with words, your will to bring ideas and thoughts to life, your nature to lead or to follow, to inspire, to analyze, to see the bigger picture, or your natural problem- solving abilities all are a part of your functions and personality.

Webster defines Function as an action performed by a device, department, or person that produces a result. You have the ability to produce results in an area of gifting. If you can perform like a teacher, never being taught how to teach. Then you have a natural function to teach and a design that helps you to fulfill that function.

If you can perform like an engineer, never being taught how to engineer. Then you have a natural function to engineer and a design that helps you to fulfill that function

If you can perform as a culinary, never being taught how to cook. Then you have a natural function to cook and a design that helps you to fulfill that function.

If you can perform like a leader, never being taught how to lead. Then you have a natural function to lead and a design that helps you to fulfill that function.

If you can perform like a fashionista, never working one day in the fashion industry. Then you have a natural function for fashion and a design that helps you to fulfill that function.

If you can perform as a beauty guru, never taking a single class on beauty. Then you have a natural function to create beauty and a design that helps you to fulfill that function.

If you can perform in a specific athletic position, without ever being taught that position. Then you have a natural function for athletics and a design that helps you to fulfill that function.

No one taught a bird how to fly. How to fly was already built into the bird because that's its natural function. Its wings, the weight of its body, and everything else that makes a bird a bird was all designed in a way that would allow the bird to fly. No one taught the fish how to function in water because how to swim was already built into the fish. Its fins, and the unique shape of its body was all designed to help the fish carry out its natural function to SWIM.

I have never taken a single public speaking class but when I speak people may assume I have a degree in public speaking, but that function was already built into me. I was designed for it. I have all the necessary functions I need to operate as a speaker. No one has to teach you what you already do naturally. Your functions are a part of your nature they make up who you are. Your functions give you the ability to operate uniquely in your area of gifting. No one taught Bill Gates how to make better software than IBM. He was already designed that way. Your DNA allow you to function the way you do, without anyone having to teach you. I have noticed over the years that when people operate in their function, they may not see it as a gift because it's something they naturally do. They never look at their function as something great or amazing. They look at it as if it's something that everyone can do, but everyone cannot do what you are capable of doing. What you see as easy others may see as hard. It's easy for you because you were born with that particular function, but people who do not have your function it's a challenge to them. Not everyone has the DNA to do mathematics, to sing, to act, to dance, to create beauty, to invent, to create fashion, to lead, and etc.... Every function that you have is designed to help you fulfill your why.

Function in your natural environment.

Your function determines your environment. A bird is its happiest not when it's in a cage or bird house eating food or on the ground where it baths, but in the air where it's allowed to use its function. The fish is its happiest when it's in water, why, because the water allows the fish to use its function. There is an environment waiting for you that you naturally belong in. If you could quit your job right now and go into an environment that would allow you to use your function where would you go to put your functions to use?

Would you go to a Classroom, or a stage?

Would you go behind a camera?

Would you go on the field?

Would you go into the kitchen?

Would you go into a hospital?

Would you go into a church?

Would you go into the lab?

Would you go into the fashion world?

Would you go into beauty and make-up?

Would you go to help the sick?

Would you go to help the homeless?

Would you go help rescue kids?

Would you go help animals?

Would you go help broken men?

Would you go help battered, women?

Would you go to a recording studio?

The Functions Inside Your DNA

You always feel your happiest and fulfilled when you are in an environment that causes you to use your functions. If you can find an environment that allows you to be yourself, you have found an environment that allows you to use your functions and to operate in your DNA.

Do me a favor, participate in these exercises with me. Participating in these exercises will help you to locate your natural functions/abilities.

Exercise 1

The function/s you were born with has equipped you with abilities that allow you to do certain things you find really easy. Do you catch yourself helping people with a particular task? It's most likely because you're great at it, whether you realize it or not. If you think about it, people have likely been telling you that you are great at something for a long time. You just weren't listening. You might think your functions are only something you're great at doing because it's a part of your nature, but sometimes our functions are the things we don't even think about. If people describe you as a creative thinker, and you are confident in those abilities to come up with new ideas, your functions will produce innovation. You can consider becoming an entrepreneur or marketing genius.

People describe my wife as a fashionista because she is confident in her visual abilities. She can see the finished product before people can even form the idea in their mind of what something will look like. This function provides her the ability to create new trends, and it also gives her an eye for anticipating what her audience will respond to next. This function gives her the ability to become a fashion designer or fashion stylist. How do people describe you when you are not around? Do they describe you as being loud, being funny, being creative, being computer savvy, being a talker, being intellectual, or being good with your hands? However, people describe you will be correlated to the functions that are inherent within you. I know I find speaking super easy, and I believe that others should find it to be just as easy, but that's not how it works in life. Instead, I find that others struggle while I stand there feeling like it's a cake walk. If there is anything that comes naturally to you that doesn't seem so natural to others, it's called a function. That's why it's critical to take a long hard look at what you do effortlessly.

Maybe you're naturally great at explaining things or giving good advice. Maybe you're naturally great at making people laugh or entertaining them using no effort at all. Maybe you're naturally great at organizing or planning, or maybe you're naturally great at drawing graphs or working with numbers. Maybe you're naturally great at singing, or acting, maybe you 're naturally great at styling or designing, or maybe you're naturally great at observing things or having an eye for beauty. Maybe you're naturally great at reporting things or telling stories, or maybe you're naturally great at writing or thinking of new things. Whatever it is, you are naturally great at something. It may be that you have never paid attention to what you are actually naturally great at.

Grab a pen and write down some things you can do naturally with little to no effort.

1. _____

_____

_____

_____

_____

Exercise 2

There are family, friends, and associates around you that get to observe you in a way that you cannot observe yourself.

Ask everyone you know that will give you an honest assessment of what they think you're naturally great at. Their insight will be valuable, informative, enlightening, endorsing and reinforcing. Their observations have greater insight than self-analysis. Ask a lot of people who know you, but always ask them one-on-one. Ask them these four questions.

1.

What makes me unique?

_____

_____

_____

_____

_____

_____

2.

What do you think I do particularly well using no effort?

_____

_____

_____

_____

_____

_____

3.

What is my strongest skill or characteristic?

_____

_____

_____

_____

_____

4.

What do you think I'm naturally good at?

_____

_____

_____

_____

_____

Compile the results, and there you will discover the function you were unaware you had.

Everything those individuals explained to you, you will notice all those things come naturally to you, and that they have always been in you since you were born. You may have never thought of them as a function, but those functions you have everyone does not have.

Exercise 3

Your functions can also be discovered in other ways. Your functions can be discovered through television shows you love and you cannot get enough of? It can be discovered through books and magazines on a particular topic that you cannot help but dig into. What you are and who you are come out of you when things like television shows and books elicit those functions you were born with. For example, those who are role models to you spark things in you because it helps you to identify traits in you they have. Those abilities that you know you have that they have causes you to try living through them as you watch them perform their functions.

1. What TV shows or movies make you think about you and excites you the most to watch?

    _____

    _____

    _____

    _____

2. What celebrities do you love the most that makes you see yourself in them?

    _____

    _____

    _____

    _____

3. Name some things you have in common with the celebrities you named, and the TV shows and movies you like.

_____

_____

_____

_____

_____

_____

After jotting down what you and your favorite celebrities have in common I hope you are now aware that you don't have to live through them when you have a similar function. The only difference between you and them is that they are aware of their functions, and they put it out there for the world to see.

Exercise 4

Think back as far as you possibly can to when you were a child. Think back to times when you weren't influenced by your environment, by your friends, teachers, peers or fears. Back to times when your parents' expectations of you didn't go outside of you playing and exploring in a safe and secure environment.

1. What did you want to be?

_____

_____

_____

_____

_____

2. How did you fill your days?

_____

_____

_____

_____

_____

3. What were your favorite things to play?

_____

_____

_____

_____

_____

4. What did you do that everyone else wish they could do?

_____

_____

_____

_____

_____

5. What did you find fun to do in your alone time?

_____

_____

_____

_____

_____

6. What did you dream of becoming?

_____

_____

_____

_____

_____

These questions express your inborn abilities. They help you to see what functions were operating in you as a child. If your favorite thing as a child was to put together puzzles, then you probably function as a natural problem solver. That's why people come to you with their problems all the time. As a kid, I loved to play games where I was the leader or teacher. Thinking back to those days, I recognize the functions I had to lead and teach were always in me. It has always been a part of who I am. To this very day, I love leading people into discovering who they are and schooling them how they can become more. Your functions have always been there you just were unaware of them.

Everyone loves to operate in their functions. I have taken notice that when people are operating in their function, they have no sense of time. Time becomes lost when you are doing things that are connected to who you are. When you find activities that are a part of your functions you become so engrossed in them that you don't think about time, eating or sleeping, you have to remind yourself to eat and sleep.

Exercise 5

In this exercise, you must identify where you lose your sense of time.

1. Where do you get lost in time? This will always point toward areas that are part of your natural functions and deep passions.

_____

_____

_____

_____

_____

_____

Exercise 6

If you only focus on what people will pay you for, and what you can become the best at then you will not be able to discover the passion you'll need to push you out of your comfort zone to achieve something great.

1. If money wasn't an issue what would you do to help better the lives of others.

_____

_____

_____

_____

_____

We must find our natural function if we want to make a difference in the lives of ourselves and others. DNA is inherent and to try to remove your function would be to significantly change who you are because your functions both inform and reveal your nature and the design of your DNA.

Chapter 5

The Design Of DNA

*Design is not just what it looks like and feels
like. Design is how it works."*

–Steve Jobs

Every living organism that you see
around you from plants to animals, and to
humans has the DNA to succeed. In the previous
chapters, we spoke about functions and how they
give you the ability to perform in your own
unique way. Well, those functions we talked
about were planted into DNA. For example, if
you were designed to sing then you have DNA
that supports that. Your voice, your windpipes,
your vocal cords, the capacity to recall tunes and

tonal sequences, the rhythm of your heartbeat, and the way you perceive melodies were all inputted into your DNA to provide you with the ability to produce a wonderful sound with your voice.

Whatever your DNA designed you to become you have the ability to be it, your DNA represents the complete make-up of who you are. Let me explain, if you possess the DNA to be a photographer to capture the wonders of life, you would have an eye for beauty and aesthetics. You would have an intellectual capacity to perceive beauty and communicate it to others in photos or words of expression. if you possess the DNA to teach, then you were born with the intellectual capacity to retain an enormous amount of information with the ability to sort and structure it in a way that you could transfer the information to anyone. You were born with a high level of communication abilities, patience, ideal productivity and an inclination to work with others. You were born to make people think. The very essence of what you are to become is reflected in your DNA.

DNA communicates what a thing does, through its built and functions.

Where you built to be creative?

Where you built to be an actor?

Where you built to do carpentry?

Where you built to be a Mechanic?

Where you built to be an organizer or planner?

Where you built to be a marketer?

Whatever it is you were built to do is correlated to your DNA.

Built inside every product is an action that produces value.

The DNA inside of every product was created to produce a certain action. That action gives the product the ability to perform its intended use. I possess speaking and teaching DNA and that DNA produces an ability to communicate in a compelling way. Therefore, my DNA designed me to speak and teach. Discovering the DNA that you carry is a vital part of understating who you are and what you are capable of becoming. Inside the DNA of every designed product is value, and that value translates into worth, and worth creates wealth.

The way you look, the color of your skin, your height, the language you speak, your physical attributes, your intellectual capacity are all a part of your DNA. Your DNA will always relate to your success, the innate, intimate part of who you are. It's what expresses the purpose of executing the reason for a thing being.

DNA will always predict the nature of a thing.

Inside the DNA every product are abilities that reflect its nature. When you were born, you were built and designed in a way that gives you the power and capacity to do that which your DNA designed you to do. How often have you sat down and thought about the natural abilities you have that make up your DNA? I guess probably not much at all or probably never. So, let me introduce you to a word I learned while searching for my DNA. The word is called Aptitude!!!! Aptitudes are natural abilities or inclinations for certain types of functions.

For example, if a child can draw a picture in his mind and bring it out in an art form, then his spatial aptitude is high. He may not already be an artist or Leonardo De Vinci, but the function or Aptitude is there. Spatial Aptitude indicates a person's ability to visualize things in space. What are your aptitudes, the natural abilities built into your DNA? Here are a few examples of aptitudes.

Were you designed with Verbal or non-verbal communications abilities?

– Can you write or speak words in a way that can transfer ideas, emotions, or information. Can you give a lecture, act out your feelings, or write poetry, because these are all methods of communication aptitude? Then you have **verbal and non-verbal communication DNA. A natural born verbal and non-verbal communication abilities**

Were you designed with Verbal comprehension abilities?

- Can you express empathetic understanding of another ideals or emotions in verbal or nonverbal communications? Can you express sympathy for a friend's problem? Do you know all the current gossip, and do you have the ability to persuade people to do things? Then you have **Verbal comprehension DNA, natural born verbal comprehensive abilities.**

Were you designed with Logical abilities?

– Can you apply thought or logic to problems with very little mental effort? Do you have the ability to see the resolution before having a solution to the problem? Do you know exactly what to do in every situation? Are you able to calculate in one's mind whether something will work or not? Then you have **Logical DNA, natural born logical abilities.**

104

Were you designed with Artistic abilities?

– Are you visually creative, do you have musical abilities or dramatic talents? Can you draw, take amazing photographs, dance, or design an outfit and apply makeup very well. Then you have **Artistic DNA, natural born artistic abilities.**

Were you designed with Mechanical abilities?

– Can you recognize the connection between parts of machines, the way things are made, and finding ways to make things work? Can you hook up a car stereo in an automobile? Can you take apart something and put it back together? Can you build a house? Then you have **Mechanical DNA and natural born mechanical abilities**.

Were you designed with Numerical abilities?

– Do you love to work with numbers? Do you like solving math problems? Do you like knowing how many miles your car gets per gallon and budgeting your finances and other finances? Then you have **Numerical DNA, and natural born numerical abilities.**

Were you designed with Clerical abilities?

– Are you always arranging and recording numbers and letter combinations? Are you always alphabetizing or putting items in a special order, filing reports, typing information, keeping records? Then you have **Clerical DNA, a natural clerical ability.**

Were you designed with Spatial abilities?

– Do you have an understanding of how parts of things fit together or multidimensional understanding? Are you able to put together a jigsaw puzzle, or rearrange furniture attractively in a room, and put together model cars? Then you have **Spatial DNA, a natural born spatial ability.**

Were you designed with Physical abilities?

– Do you have bodily strength and coordination, manual dexterity? Do you love playing sports, lifting weights, moving furniture, and building things? Then you have **Physical DNA, and natural born physical abilities**.

Were you designed with Organizational abilities?

– Do you like implementing and evaluating actions for yourself or others? Do you like planning a party, promoting a party, planning a vacation, marketing and conducting events? Then you have **Organizational DNA, a natural born organizational ability.**

Were you born with Intellectual abilities?

- Are you a creative thinker, fast learner, a forward thinker, and a developer of concepts. Do you like teaching, studying, reading, finding new ways to do things, and developing plans to increase the value of something? Then you have **Intellectual DNA, and natural born Intellectual abilities.**

These aptitudes or abilities built into our DNA will manifest more as we develop and learn the Laws of our DNA. Every created thing was intended to operate by certain laws and once you learn those laws you learn the success that those laws produce. If you learn the laws of your workplace, your business, or relationships you will find that they produce success if you follow them; and you also will find that they produce failure when you violate them. If you were to put corn syrup in your gas tank instead of gasoline you would have violated the Law that it takes to make the car run. You have to follow the built in Laws of the product if you want it to succeed. That's why a manual is needed with every created product, because It explains the do's and don'ts (the laws) to guarantee the products success.

What Are Laws

Laws are established principles meaning they will work the same way every single time for anyone who gets involved. For instance, gravity is a natural law it works the same way for everyone. If the Law of Gravity did not exist then what you throw into the air would just float, but since the Law of Gravity is a real thing than what you throw into the air or off a building will be pulled down by gravity. This law will work the same way every single time no matter how big, or small something is. Laws represent established natural patterns within creation. Everything you were created to be is a finished product in the form of a seed guided by laws to ensure success. You have inside you all the characteristics and capabilities you will ever need to become what your DNA designed you to be. In fact, every created thing started out as a seed. Every human, plant, and animal God/universe created were given the ability to multiply and replenish according to the laws established within that product. You were constructed for continuous success. That success is wrapped in a seed form

110

that must be planted and taken through established laws to grow and develop to fully produce its success. Everything you are designed to become starts in a seed form so for you to become who you were designed to be you must follow the laws of a seed.

The Laws of Every Seed

Law 1

A seed must be placed in the right environment for it to begin its process of becoming what it's DNA designed it to be.

Your DNA will only begin to succeed in the environment in which it was designed for, it cannot produce in a place it was never designed to be. If you are in the wrong environment, your DNA will not be able to produce success. That could be why you are not seeing the success you are hoping for. To prevent ending up in a constant cycle of failure you have to place yourself in the right environment to maximize your success. Buckminster Fuller, an American neo-futuristic architect, said it perfectly: "Everyone is born a genius, but the process of living de-geniuses them. Whatever company environment you are in, there's a certain DNA or talent that is valued. If you happen to have DNA that aligns with the company's, then you will rise to the top quickly. I once worked at a car dealership where you had to have some type of sales ability. If you were persuasive and had communication DNA, then you were the most-coveted. Product specialist however was seen as important but not the most-coveted or critical for the company's success. If you were a product specialist with no sales DNA than overcoming objections and rejections would be very hard for you to maximize your performance in that specific environment, but if you were great at persuading and communicating then you would excel within that environment.

The same thing happens in companies, schools, organizations and households everywhere. For this reason, you need to find the environment in which your DNA fits. The bottom line is that the environment you place yourself in will either develop your DNA or trap your DNA. It's my guess that if you are reading this book then you would like to mature your DNA. So, place yourself in an environment that can develop your DNA. A shark in a fish tank will grow eight inches, but in the ocean, it will grow eight feet or more. The shark will never outgrow its environment and the same is true about you. You must find your soil. If you think you possess the DNA to teach than find an environment that's capable of producing teachers and plant yourself in that soil.

Law 2

For a seed to become a tree, it must isolate itself.

A seed must take itself away from the earth and hide in the ground. How often are you hiding yourself to refine your DNA? How often do you go away from everyone to seek and find out who you really are? How often do you isolate yourself to read the necessary books on your function and listen to the essential lectures to develop your DNA? You have to learn to get away to spend time with yourself. You have to get to know you better, and the only way to do that is giving yourself some space. If you pack your life with so many tasks and activities daily, you will have no time to breathe let alone get to know yourself. You cannot become a victim of a schedule that won't allow you to develop who you are. You need space so that you can focus,

114

inspire, and excite yourself about discovering your DNA. You cannot do this being bombarded by life.

Law 3

For a seed to become a tree, it must die. You have to learn discipline.

If you cannot die to things that stop your DNA from releasing its abilities how will you ever succeed in life. You must learn to die to self, to old friends, to old habits, to old behaviors, to old associations, and to old environments. If you don't learn to deny yourself of the things that hinder you, you will never see the real potential of your DNA. As long as the person you are continues to live you cannot become any better. You must die for a new you to be born. The old you in the new you cannot exist at the same time. The only way to accomplish your goals, plans, and aspirations is to become something different.

If you could achieve your dreams without being something different, then there would be no need to change. Change comes because you know in order to accomplish your goals you have to become someone different. Nothing changes until you change. If you refuse to grow then nothing will change in your life, so you have to make up your mind. Do you want to become something different or stay the same?

I was always taught that mathematics has to be applied to your life in order for development to take place. If there is no adding and subtracting in your life, then you are not changing or becoming any different. What are you adding to your life that is causing you to grow and become more? What are you subtracting from your life that is hindering you from growing and becoming more? If you are poor and choose to stay surrounded by a circle of poor people, please tell me how they can help you to become wealthy and influential.

Law 4

For a seed to become a tree, it must be germinated.

You have to find people and things that are going to stretch you, develop you, and push you. You have to listen to lectures, talks, and find books because they all play a part in germinating you. You have to get around people who make you dream big, think big, and talk big. You have to commit yourself after reading this chapter to be around people who will germinate you.

Law 5

For a seed to become a tree, you have to water it.

You have to water your seed that means you have to develop some habits and routines to do daily to improve yourself. What are you doing every day on a daily basis to become more? You have to put yourself on some type of plan. I plan monthly to read at least three books and listen to at least five lectures in the area that fits my DNA. How often are you studying and practicing your area of gifting? My daughter is 15 years old, and she has wanted to be an actor since she was five years of age. Every week she chooses a monologue out of a movie, and she studies the character of that person, and she presents to us the reenactment every Sunday. I have noticed by her doing this she has become so much greater.

She continuously waters her seed. What are you doing to water your seed?

Law 6

For a seed to become a tree, it has to have fertilizer.

You have to refine and refresh yourself daily to continue growing your DNA. You are not going to refine yourself by hanging around people who contaminate you and bring poison into your life. Yea, those around you may be great people, and you may love them, but the direction they may have you going is not a part of your DNA. Don't allow yourself to be deceived. The people around you are affecting you. You have to put yourself in the midst of people like you who are going for what you are going for so that you can learn and develop. That's why it's critical for you to choose your association. Have you ever heard the saying birds of a feather flock together? Eagles do not hang with pigeons, owls do not hang with hawks. Eagles associate with other eagles because they help to develop one another. A pigeon cannot develop an eagle. If your DNA designed you to dance and all you associate with is computer engineers, you will never grow to become the dancer your DNA designed you to be. You must associate yourself with individuals that can develop your DNA not hinder it. Who are you allowing to fertilize you? People are fertilizing you rather you believe it or not. If you continue to hang around bad company and people who are never going anywhere, it will eventually affect you. They will begin to pollute your life, and before you know it, you will be on the path to disaster.

Law 7

For a seed to become a tree it needs sunshine.

You need external influence in your life to help you develop your seed into a fruit. What seminars have you attended on your DNA that's outside of your normal comfort zone? What influences outside of your circle do you associate with that can help develop your DNA. What networks are you a part of that causes your DNA to grow more? You must have external influences outside of your circle of influence so that they can help your design develop from new perspectives.

Law 8

For a seed to become a tree, it needs time

You need time to develop; you cannot rush what you are to become. It's a process that happens over time. Time helps you to develop to

121

the point of greatness. If you were just to jump into who your DNA designed, you to become you would miss all the lessons and development that it took to get there along the way. Therefore, your foundation would be so frail the smallest problems would cause you to collapse. When you lack patience, you look for instant gratification, and when you look for instant gratification, you will always become discouraged because you find out that nothing just happens right away. A seed needs time to bear fruit. Just like the development of you will take time it doesn't happen overnight, and if you lose sight of that, it could stop your functions from releasing its DNA. I know you might not want to continue to do what you're doing. I know you might not want to finish reading this book or study the area of your DNA, but if you continue, you will guarantee your success. Remember when you follow the laws of a thing you guarantee its success. You must never despise small beginnings because they teach you a lot along the way. Small beginnings help you to build a strong foundation because the lessons that you learn on your journey teach you how to withstand the inevitable pressure of life. You become like a tree when it is fully developed no matter the weather or the season it stands firm and cannot be removed, and that's what you are designed to become when you develop yourself as a tree and deliver your fruit.

Chapter 6

Success Begins In the Mind

If you truly believe in your mind that your DNA designed you to succeed than your thoughts will forge into reality what your mind believes.

What your DNA designed you to become will be affected by the way you think. Everything you have on the inside of you will remain trapped if your thoughts are trapped. The way you think can lead you away from your DNA and it's ultimately responsible for what you become. Where you currently are in life is based on the way you have been conditioned to think. If you have been conditioned to think in a successful way you will become successful, but if you have been conditioned to think you will fail then chances are you will fail. The condition of your thought determines the condition of your life. If you want to change the condition of your life, you have to change the condition of your thoughts. You will never lose weight keeping the same mindset about food and exercising. Your thoughts are the most powerful resource you have in your possession. You can have all the talent in the world but if your thoughts don't allow you to operate in the capacity of your design, then your functions or talents will mean nothing.

All that you DNA designed you to become will be a direct result of how you think. Yes, you are engineered to become something wonderful, but your ability to achieve great things in life lies within the power of your thoughts. You must learn to win this war going on between your ears.

Your life is a reflection of your thoughts

Your thought determines how you feel, and how you feel determines the decision you make. The decision you make determines your actions, and your actions determine your habits. Your habits determine your character, and your character determines your destination in life. The moment you think you're not designed to become something is the moment you begin to feel that way. Once you start feeling that way you begin to make a decision based on how you feel. Those decisions lead to actions that lead you away from becoming what you are designed to be. Those actions lead to habits that create a character that's not you. Once you become something, you are not you arrive at a place that isn't designed for you to succeed. So, if you want to change your destination in life, you have to change your character. In order to change your character, you have to change your habit. To change your habit, you have to change your actions. To change your actions, you have to change your decision. To change your decision, you have to change the way you feel. To change the way you feel, you have to change your thoughts. Your life is a reflection of your thoughts. The reality that you are currently shaping at this moment in your thought life is determining your future. Everything you experience in the outside world has originated from your thoughts. I remember reading a story about three men who were digging a hole and as they were digging, they were asked the question.

What are you doing?

The first man replied digging up dirt.

The second man replied, working to pay my bills.

The third man replied building a water well that will permit thousands of people to drink clean water and eliminate disease caused by bacteria from dirty water.

The first man saw nothing, the second man saw a way to pay his bills, and the third person saw what the project was designed to become. He saw the work as it would be not as it was. He saw the benefit that it would bring to people. He saw a finished product so who do you think had the better mindset. All three people were doing the same thing, but only one could see what was to come, he saw the finished product before it was done.

Your thought will always interpret what you see and hear

The power of your mind can cause you to have a different experience than the person sitting right next to you. What a person sees and hears is small compared to how he/she thinks. Because the way someone thinks determines

129

what they see and hear. Their perception of a thing is based on their thoughts. Your thoughts will always interpret what you see and hear. Many times, people think their circumstances control the way they feel, not knowing that the way they think has created the circumstance. The problems, the struggles, your current situations, all reflect your mindset. You are where you are because of your thoughts rather wanted or unwanted. Your thought power creates your reality.

When I manage a group of sales consultants, I would give out performance-based bonuses. Some would be excited, and others would be disappointed. I did not get it at the time but thinking back to it I understand why some would be excited and why others would not be as excited. Every one of them started off at the same starting line, but in that room, were those who thought they could win the bonus money and those who thought they could not earn the bonus money. The ones who thought they could win would be excited about bonus money. Those who thought they could not win would leave out of the meeting being negative. Your thoughts interpret your reality.

The success that you wish to see right now is at your disposal, but you must learn to align your thinking with your DNA to become who you are designed to be

If a great opportunity smacked a negative person in the face, they would still think negatively about it because they got smacked. The cup will be half full or half empty based on your thoughts. I never look at a problem as a problem. I look at it as an opportunity to grow and develop. It would not be a problem if I knew how to fix it before it became a problem. It's a problem because it's there to teach me something

I don't know. It's there to stretch me. That's how I think about every issue. I know there are millions of people out there that would not dare to think this way and those my friends are the people who never get ahead in life. Inside of you lay dormant abilities beyond your imagination, but they can only become accessible through your thought life. The success that you wish to see right now is at your disposal, but you must learn to align your thinking with your DNA to become who you are designed to be. A great friend of mine has a kid that has been drafted by the Tennessee Titan. His name is Dylan Dawkins. Though-out life Dylan's abilities have been challenged. He was always told he was too small to play running back and that he would not be successful if he continued trying to play that position. Many people thought he would not make it, but at every level from elementary to college, he has proven them wrong. He never once thought he was too small. Dylan would go-head on with people twice his size and make it through them. No matter what they thought about him, he never thought about himself. That's why he has succeeded at every level, and I'm pretty sure he will do the same in the NFL. He thinks differently. I remember people constantly saying those exact words to me in the workplace. They would say to me you are not like the others. When they spoke those words, I knew they really meant that I thought differently.

You must choose to think different

Those who you see on television or read about in magazines all thought differently than the people around them. In order to become different, you have to think differently. If you think like everyone around you, you will become no different. I made it out of poverty, out of the projects, out of being a statistic because I thought differently. I remember my mother traveling to churches to get boxes of food so that we would

133

have food to eat. I thought at that moment in my life as a young boy if I ever had kids they would never have to endure what I have. I never thought like the people around me. I always thought differently. Some of the friends I grew up with are dead or in prison for the remainder of their life. They chose not to think differently. I made it out because I did. I know that you cannot hear the passion in my voice at the moment, but if you are reading this book, I'm telling you that it is possible for you to think differently in an environment that tries to condition you to think you will never make it out. If I can become successful and climb out of a hole so deep in poverty, you too can. By choosing to think differently, I changed the course of my life. You have to start thinking about what you think about, or you will hold hostage the very person your DNA designed you to become. Your thoughts become a reality. Everything you lay eyes on in this world has originated from somebody's mind.

They saw it in their inner thoughts and then made it a reality. To become what your DNA designed you to be, you must learn to control the nature of your inner dominating, thoughts. By doing this, you will attract what you wish to see in your life and without doing this you will attract the things you hate the most. Everything you desire to see come true in your life is only a thought away. All you have to do is think it into existence. Every thought you think is either shaping your life the way you want it or shaping a life that you will despise. Either way, your thoughts are forging your reality.

I was doing some research online and came across a case study done by Psychologists Ulrich Weger and Stephen Loughnan. The case study entails them asking two groups of people to answer questions. The people in one group were told that before each question the answer would quickly flash on their screens but that it

135

would flash too quickly for them to consciously perceive, but slow enough for their unconscious to take in. The other group was told that the flashes simply signaled the next question. But in all actuality for both groups a random string of letters flashed across their screens not the answers. But the people who thought the answers were flashed did better on the test. Expecting to know the answer made people more likely to get the answer right. When you cause your mind to believe something it tries to forge into reality that belief. If you sincerely believe in your mind that your DNA designed you in a specific way to make sure you succeeded in your area of gifting, then your thoughts will forge into reality what your mind believes. When your mind believes something, it causes your thoughts to create actions and those actions, compel you to behave in a certain way that will begin shaping into reality what you believe.

Be aware of fraudulent thoughts

Well, you might be saying to yourself if it was that easy why isn't everyone successful. I'm sure no one starts out in life believing they can't do something, and you are right. Once the mind believes it can achieve something a fraudulent thought comes along that destroys that belief. There's a fraud that exists within your thoughts that's trying to shape a reality of its own. He's there to steal your dreams to kill your confidence and dismantle your hope. He's the silent voice that whispers many things in your thoughts like you don't have what it takes. You are not going to make it. What makes you think you can do that? You're not smart enough. You can't start your own business. No one's going to give you an opportunity. You don't have enough talent. No one's going to like you. You are going to fail. You're never going to succeed. Why try this and you know it's not going to work. He's

137

the fraud that instills fear into your life helping you to form negative thoughts about what your DNA designed you to become. The fraud in your mind is a parasite. Those fraudulent thoughts eat away at every positive thought. They destroy your excitement and energy. They eat away at your desire to accomplish something great. The fraud's job is to make sure your thought life remains negative. As a matter of fact, it feeds on negativity. It loves for you to hang around people that discourage you. Those fraudulent thoughts are there to make you second guess yourself. Those thoughts are there to constantly remind you that you don't have the experience. That people are not going to be satisfied with your services, and that you lack the ability to become something you are not.

To stop the fraud from destroying your life you have to become aware of when it speaks to you. You have to know that the moment you believe something, coming right behind that belief is the fraud. You must not allow those fraudulent thoughts to talk you out of what you believe. Recognize when it speaks and silence it right away by stating out loud that I can, and I will move forward on what I believe. The more you continue to speak out loud what you believe the fraud will disappear from your thought life. It's very important to guard your thought life because in those thoughts exist everything you are to become.

Your thoughts can place limitations on your DNA.

You cannot allow your thoughts to set limitations on what you can become. I have watched so many people who are amazingly gifted permit their thoughts to limit the expansion of their abilities. It's like their thoughts convinced them that they are only good using

139

their DNA in certain areas. When they have the capabilities to use them far beyond the current limits they place on themselves. Those people allow their secondary thoughts to tell them they will not be good at doing something their DNA designed them to do. When they have the DNA to do it. Their thoughts convinced them not to operate outside of their comfort zone. When you do not allow yourself to jump into new things that will cause you to get uncomfortable your thoughts become a limitation to all that you can become. You can never know what you can grow to be if you don't travel down all the roads that are connected to your DNA. If it's a part of your DNA and you are naturally gifted at it, and you don't allow yourself to do it because your thoughts cause you to fear failing or getting uncomfortable than you my friend are limiting yourself. The only way to lift the limitations your mind places on you is to do something different, to do something that you never tried before, and to do something that makes you uncomfortable as long as it's aligns with your DNA. Try something out of the norm that allows you to use your functions and operate within your DNA.

Your brain gives birth to what it can conceive.

What your DNA designed you to become is first conceived within the mind. Everything that you will be is born out of your mind. Once you start thinking, conception begins to take place and conception once conceived within the mind gives birth to a brainchild. Ford Motor Co. is Henry Ford's brainchild. It was born out of his mind. Google is Larry Page and Sergey Brin brainchild. It was born out of their minds. What brainchild are you giving birth to? What you are to become is conceived within your mind. You can never give birth to something your mind never designs. Your mind is the designer of your future. What you want to become, what you want to do and what you want to accomplish is all designed within your mind.

Chapter 7

You Must Plan Your Success

Planning is bringing the future into the present so that you can do something about it now

- Alan Lakein

The outcomes that you want to experience in life are built on the plans that you have and do not have. If you do not plan to succeed, then you plan to fail. Your success in life will be found in the plans you have. You have to plan to become what your DNA designed you to be. Poof does not happen in the life of successful people. Planning got them to where they are. Who you are and what you are to become will only happen with a plan. A motion does not happen unless there is movement. How can you expect a better future if you don't plan it?

You have to plan your success.

There was a bright young man that planned the success of his future while in elementary school. As a child in elementary school, he planned to become an entrepreneur. He started by working in his grandfather's grocery store to create for himself some working capital to invest. He took that money he earned from his grandfather's grocery store and all of the other jobs to buy some stock. At 11 years old, he made his first investment, buying three shares of Cities Service Preferred at $38 per share. By the age of 13, he started a few businesses. He sold cold drinks, weekly magazines, stamps, chewing gum and went door to door delivering newspapers and selling his own horse racing tip sheets. That same year he filed a tax return on all of the income he earned and used his bicycle as a write-off.

During his time in high school, he partnered up with a friend in the two bought a pinball machine and installed it in a barbershop. That pinball machine generated enough income to buy two more pinball machines, and they also installed them in barbershops. They eventually sold the business for $1200. His interest in investing and plans to become wealthy did not stop there. He went on to college to earn a Master of Science in Economics. He then went on to sell securities for Buffett-Falk & Company for three years, then worked for his mentor for two years as an analyst at Graham-Newman Corp. While working for his mentor he forms a firm called Buffett Partnership Ltd in his hometown. Utilizing the methods that he learned from his

146

mentor Benjamin Graham. These methods led him to become successful at identifying undervalued companies. That ability translated into millions. Thus, becoming the person today, you know as Warren Buffett.

Plans are roadmap they help you to see where you are going and how to get there.

Everything Warren Buffett has become he chose to become by planning to become it. A plan will map out things you must do to achieve the life you want as well as the things you must not do to accomplish the life you want. If you have a vision with no plan, then how do you expect the images you see of your future to become a reality. Let me let you in on a little secret. Nothing just happens, let me repeat it, nothing just happens. If you want things to happen, you have to make it happen. Whatever you plan to be or not be you will be.

A plan is vital to the success that you see in life it's an essential key without it you will not succeed.

Every successful person planned to be where they currently are in their life. Where I am today in my life is because I planned it. I planned to become an author otherwise you would not be reading this book. Every speech I have ever given I planned. Everything I have accomplished so far in my life I've planned. Where you are now is where you planned to be rather it's something you are enjoying or not enjoying. A plan is like a roadmap. It shows you how to get to a specific destination. It creates a map for you on the road of life. If where you are now in life is not where you would like to be than map out a different destination. A plan makes you aware of where you are and where you are going. When using a navigation system to find a particular destination, that navigation first shows you where you are located, and it then gives you the best directions on how to get to where you are going.

On your way to your destination, you will find that there are multiple roads designed to get you to your destination. Some of those roads may be performing construction, and if you happen to travel one that's under construction, it will cause you to take a detour. In life, you will have detours because nothing is ever perfect. Expect detour on the road to developing your DNA. If you lose your job, you are just on a detour. If you cannot get the money to start a business, you are just on a detour. If you are filing bankruptcy, you are on a detour. If things keep getting in the way of your business plans you are just on a detour. You must know that plans may change, the road to get to your destination may change, but the destination itself doesn't change. A plan is the navigation to life; it gives you directions to get to your destination, the future you. You cannot become the future you without a plan. Are you planning to set free the man or women that is trapped on the inside of you? Are you planning to see what you are able to become? Life will always test your plans. That's why you have to plan how you will win before you pick the fight.

You will be naive to think trouble won't come your way on your road to success.

Every person I know who has made it in life found trouble on their journey. You will find problems on your journey. When you have a plan to win despite the trouble that finds you, you will never be defeated. People without a plan will never win. You will find in life that the ones without a plan will become poor because they don't plan their profit. They don't plan to do anything productive; they plan nothing at all. There are thousands of people living on the streets as I write this book and most of them are great people, but where they are they planned to be. The people who never plan anything always think that things and situations will work out, but things will never work out. Instead, things work you out and once they work you out the result will not be anything you planned. Whatever you want to become you have to plan to become. Success is always waiting for a plan so that it can bring into reality a future that doesn't exist.

Webster defines a plan as a method worked out in advance for achieving some objective.

A plan provides you with the ability to give meaning to time. Time will always exist as long as you live, but when a purpose is applied to time, time now has meaning. When you give meaning to time, it allows you to determine its use. Those who decide not to apply purpose to time are those who go with the flow of life and choose the way of poverty. Those who choose to become successful have 24 hours a day, and those who choose to remain in poverty have 24 hours a day. What is the major difference between the two? Time, the successful apply purpose to time the poor just lives in time. The successful produces something in time while the poor produces nothing in time but instead lives off what the successful produce in their allotted time.

Those who want to become what they were born to be must apply purpose to time. The only way to impact your life and generation starts with giving meaning to time.

Think about the successful people around you. How often do you see them waste time? That's because their time has purpose and meaning. Now think about the people that are around you who are unsuccessful. How often do they waste their time? Probably all the time because their time has no meaning and no purpose attached. Successful people give meaning and purpose to unused time. What do you plan on doing with the next 24 hours that you have not used? People who want to become successful already know the answer to that question. Individuals who are not looking to become successful are not concerned with such a question. Every day of my life I plan to do something that helps me to become successful. Rather that's reading a book, attending an event, studying my craft or connecting with people that can help me to become more. You will never become the person you see in the future without giving purpose to time.

Whoever controls your time controls your future. If a job controls your time, it controls your future. If television controls your time, it will control your future. If hanging out controls your time, it will control your future. If nothing controls your time, then nothing will be in your future. If a plan controls your time, then you will become exactly what you planned.

Without a plan, you will never be able to take charge of your future.

Inside of you is something greater than you can imagine. The future is not outside of you, it's inside of you. You are the inventor of your future. Everything I am today I predicted to become because I made plans to become it. Whatever you plan to be you will become. Whatever you don't plan to become, you will be. If you plan to become nothing you, well you probably should finish the sentence. Every successful person predicted their future because they invented it. Yes, you can predict the future with a plan.

Phil Knight predicted his future long before he started to live it.

Enrolling as a graduate of the School of Business at Stanford University he took a small business class. While attending class, the professor assigned the class a task in which the students had to invent a new business. Knight mapped out a blueprint for a shoe company dealing specifically in sports. From this assignment, he drafted a paper titled "Can Japanese Sports Shoes Do To German Sports Shoes What Japanese Cameras Did to German Cameras. It was in writing that paper that he discovered the Design of his DNA. Graduating in 1962 with an MBA he decided not to waste any time and set sail on a trip to Japan. While in Japan he traveled to a manufacturing plant named Onitsuka. He discovered that the company created a tiger brand running shoe. Impressed by the quality of the shoe he secured a distribution deal with Onitsuka. Excited about his new venture, he returned home and immediately secured a job at an accounting firm to fund his business plan. Figuring that he might need a little more security he formed a partnership with his former Coach Bill Bowerman, establishing Blue Ribbon Sports in 1964. The two eventually quit their jobs and went hard to work on their business. Opening up a couple retails stores in Santa Monica, California, and Eugene, Oregon.

The well thought out plan allowed Knight and Bowerman in the 1960's to enjoy the fruits of their labor. However, in the early 1970's a dispute broke out between Knight, Bowerman and their distributor Onitsuka. That dispute pushed Knight and Bowerman to start their own manufacturing plant. During the startup of the new distribution center, an employee and good friend of Knight suggested naming the new company Nike after the Greek winged goddess of victory. That day Nike was Born. Knight planned from the very beginning to be the world's top designer in athletics products. Today Nike is considered as the world's largest supplier and manufacturer of athletic shoes and apparel. According to Forbes Nike brand value is about 15.9 billion dollars.

Everything Knight became he planned to be; it wasn't by luck it was by planning. Planning is a necessity of success. It's vital to you becoming more and its essential to you fulfilling your potential.

Planning impacts your life on so many levels. Planning helps you to determine the use of your resources. For example, your time, your money, your talent, your energy, your gifts, your knowledge, your house, your car, all of these are examples of your resources and planning determine the use of those resources. When you

157

have a plan in place, you will not allow your resources to be abused. When you have a plan for your money, you will not allow it to be given away to people that won't help you fulfill your purpose. You won't waste your time playing taxi with people who cannot help you get to the next level. A plan won't let you spend hours upon hours talking with someone that can't help you succeed. A plan will not allow you to waste your energy on things that cannot help you become more. If you don't control your time, your things, your life, then other people will control your future.

The greatest act of faith in vision is a plan.

I am a firm believer that if you believe in something, you execute. That which you do not believe in you don't execute. For example, if I believe I could fly then I would climb to the top of a building and jump off, but since I do not believe that I can fly or that wings will pop out of my back, then I don't jump. Whatever you believe, you will do. Whatever you don't believe, you will not do. That's why a plan shows your belief in something because a plan compels you to execute what you believe. A plan is necessary to bring into reality what you believe

A plan in something helps you to eliminate hope. I don't know if you have taken notice of this, but hopeful people are always broke, because they continually hope. They hope things will happen instead of planning for things to happen. Have you ever been around a person that said I hope we own a house one day but they're still renting? I hope I get married someday, but they're still searching. I hope I become successful someday, but they're still sitting on the couch. I hope I can start a business one day, but they're still working for an employer. Please don't misunderstand me. Hope is a great thing because it helps you to establish belief but hope by itself is completely empty so from today forward no more hoping and wishing, write down a plan.

It's time to turn your thoughts into reality.

I once heard Jim Rohn say that it's ok to think but not to be just a thinker, it's ok to have a philosophy but not to be just a philosopher, and it's okay to dream but not to be just a dreamer. You have to have a daily objective for your life, or you will be considered just a thinker, a dreamer, a hoper, or a wisher and those people never accomplish anything. Dreams don't change your life; hope doesn't change your life, wishing doesn't change your life, plans change your life. Make a commitment today to no longer be a thinker, a dreamer, a hoper, or wisher, but a planner, a doer, and executor. Do not go to sleep tonight without creating for yourself an objective for your unused time. You must learn to finish

160

the day before you start it. When you wake up with an objective, you have finished the day.

Your vision and dreams are real, but your plans will make them a reality. Your dreams want to become a reality, but they cannot become a reality without you first having a plan.

162

Chapter 8

The Work In Your DNA

Doing what your DNA designed you to do will be you fulfilling your work.

Webster defines work as an activity involving mental or physical effort done in order to achieve a purpose or result. Your DNA designed you with abilities that give you the capacity mentally and physically to achieve a purpose or successful results. Your DNA is connected to your work and your work is what you were born to complete. There is no educational system or class that can teach you how to become something your DNA designed you to be. There is no system that can teach you how to achieve your life's purpose, or at least one has not yet been created. The more aware you become of your DNA, the more you begin to discover your work. Throughout life, we have been taught that work is something we do, not something our DNA designed us for. Once you find what it is that your DNA designed you to do, you never stop working. Have you ever heard someone say that if you do what you love, then you will never work another day in your life? This statement resonates being yourself and following your own unique DNA. When you are doing what you love, you are being yourself. When your work allows you to be yourself, it will never feel like work. Have you ever heard anyone say that they love doing something they hate? The answer is probably no. People are not fulfilled in their jobs because they are continuously becoming something their DNA never designed them to be.

When you believe that work is something you do versus something you are then you will continue doing things that you dislike. You cannot continue to look for an activity that has nothing to do with your DNA. It just becomes a waste of time trying to become something you were never meant to be. You cannot allow a job to trap your work. So many people allow this to happen that's why they are depressed every Monday going to a job that doesn't help them to fulfill their DNA. Are you trapped on a job that does not allow you to become who you were designed to be?

Do you continue to go to a place that is not you?

I don't want you to take this as if I am saying jobs are a bad thing, in fact, the last job I had prepared me for my work because it allowed me to operate in my DNA. It allowed me to

165

develop my speaking and teaching DNA. So, every now and then your work will create your job. I found this to be so with my wife. She worked as the General Manager of a shoe and clothing store. This job allowed her to express her design for fashion and beauty. This led her to start a beauty blog and that led her to creating a cosmetics company which has become very successful. One of the reason for her success is her she finding the thing that connected to her to her DNA and she tells me all the time it never feels like work although she works all day. Your future is in your work. Think beyond your job.

Ask yourself these questions. Is the job you at helping you to develop your DNA? Is it helping you to develop your work and what your DNA designed you to become? Your job should be helping you develop your DNA, not to develop who you are not to become. Do not waste your time in a place that does not help you to become what your DNA designed you to be.

Your DNA can never be fired.

Your job is what they pay you to do. Your job is your skill. Your work is your natural function, something your DNA designed you for. A skill is something you learn, but DNA is inherent not something learned. You can also be replaced by someone else with the same learned skill. In other words, they can always fire you from a job, but they can never fire or lay you off from being yourself. When you leave a job, you take your work, your innate abilities, functions, and DNA, with you. Steve Jobs was fired by the very company he co-founded, but he was not fired from his work his own unique DNA.

In his renowned speech at Stanford graduating class of 2005, Jobs admitted he "really didn't know what to do for a few months.

He added, "I felt that I had let the previous generation of entrepreneurs down, that I had dropped the baton as it was being passed to me." "I even thought about running away from (Silicon) Valley. But something slowly began to dawn on me. I still loved what I did. The turn of events at Apple had not changed that one bit, and so, I decided to start over." He did just that. He went right back into operating in his unique DNA and co- founded a new computer company called NeXT, and he also launched Pixar Animation Studios. His work, his unique DNA followed him. As both companies began to see success, they became acquired. NeXT was purchased by Apple and Pixar was purchased by Disney. Apple knew that acquiring NeXT would help return Steve Jobs to the already struggling company at the time. One year after the purchase of NeXT Steve Jobs became Apple's CEO taking the struggling company back to success creating the iPod, iPhone, and iPad. Your work will be found in your DNA. When you do what your DNA designed you for nothing can stop your success

Jobs put it this way in the remaining part of his speech.

"I didn't see it then, but it turned out that getting fired from Apple was the best thing that could have ever happened to me. The heaviness of being successful was replaced by the lightness of being a beginner again, less sure about everything. It freed me to enter into one of the most creative periods of my life," Steve Jobs Stated. "I'm pretty sure none of this would have happened if I hadn't been fired from Apple. It was awful tasting medicine, but I guess the patient needed it. Sometimes life hits you in the head with a brick. Don't lose faith. I'm convinced the only thing that kept me going was that I loved what I did. You've got to find what you love." Wherever you go, you can plant your natural

169

abilities so that it can start to prosper you again. You are much more than your job than the place you work at. Nobody can fire you from that. Having a job is a great thing but finding your true work is everything. As you can see in the statement given about Steve Jobs. This book is designed to shift your thinking so that you can find yourself. Because when you find yourself, you will gain a new perspective on what you were created to do on this earth instead of just being reactive to your environment. You were not created just to punch a clock you were created to fulfill a purpose. You were created to contribute to your generation. The functions you were born with are built into your DNA, so that you can make a difference in the world. The world needs you. The people you see every day need you—and you need them. You may not know what's in you yet, but I hope this book brings it out. The innate abilities, your functions were given to you to fulfill your purpose, your why for existing. Fulfilling your purpose can happen wherever you go. Your work is ongoing, throughout your life on this earth. Your job is only your career a small portion of your life because it is temporary. You can lose your job tomorrow. Your whole career can end today, but your work is something that you will have to complete until the very day you die. It will not matter how many times you move around; you will still have what you were born with. It does not matter if you have been abused, neglected or mistreated, you still carry what you were born with on the inside of you. Your DNA cannot be worn out; it cannot be dismissed nor taken away because it's you. For your work to leave you would mean that you no longer exist. You DNA designed you in a specific way for a specific reason. When you discover your work, and how you were born to function, you will find that reason. Your Job is not your work, so you must pay close attention to this difference so that you

171

can start to discover your real work, your true functionality whether or not it happens in the context of your job environment or not.

Let me explain what I mean. Do me a favor, picture yourself having a job as a coach and that you are very successful at coaching. Imagine people telling you daily that you are an amazing coach. Does that mean coaching is an innate ability of yours and your true work? Not precisely but having the ability to inspire and help people discover their potential is. Your DNA designed you in a way that enables you to inspire and help people discover their potential which supports your job of being a coach. Your work is your ability to help people become more rather it be through writing a book, speaking or teaching.

Let me give you another example. Let's say you are a physician? Does that mean that being a doctor is something your DNA designed

172

you to be? No, but it is your job although, underneath your position, you may find your gifts of benevolence, empathy, compassion, and serving. Let's say you never became a doctor, but rather had spent all of your life volunteering to help those in need. You could have expressed that same innate ability that same inherent DNA. Your work is benevolence, empathy, and compassion for serving others.

You are defined by your work.

You are defined by your work, and your work is directly related to your DNA that's why your functions reveal who you are. An apple seed is revealed by its ability to become a tree. A bird is revealed by its ability to fly. That's why when a bird is flying it is working; It's operating within its DNA. When a seed starts to become a tree, it is working; it's fulfilling the design of its DNA. Just as a bird is defined by flying and a fish is defined by swimming so are you defined by your work (by your DNA).

For example, when you think of LeBron James, you think of a basketball player. When he is on the court, he is working; he's doing what his DNA designed him to do. When you think of TD Jakes or Joel Osteen, you think of preacher, pastor, great speaker. When they are standing at the podium teaching the Word of God, they are working doing what their DNA designed them to do. When you think of Beyoncé, you think of music. When she's creating music or recording in the studio or on stage performing; she's working doing what her DNA designed her to do. When you think of Tyler Perry you think of movies and plays. When he is directing and creating movies and plays; he is working doing what his DNA designed him to do. All of the above people are defined by their work.

The moment I stated those names you immediately identified them by their work, by what their DNA designed them to become. When people think of you, what do they think about? How do they identify you? When I'm teaching people how to identify their DNA and when I'm on stage giving a lecture to help people discover who they are, I'm working. Writing this book is me fulfilling my work. It's me doing what my DNA designed me to do.

Chapter 9

The Contribution Of Your DNA

When you cease to make a contribution, you begin to die.

-Eleanor Roosevelt

Your contribution to your generation ultimately becomes your purpose. It becomes the meaning of your existence. How your DNA made you to function, equipped you with all the abilities you will ever need to make an impact on your generation. You were born to make a difference that's why you fill a void and purposelessness when you are not contributing to society. That void compels you to ask yourself questions like, why am I here? What was I created for? What is my purpose? Does my life have meaning? Your purpose is your unique contribution to the world. All the DNA that you host on the inside of you were given to you to serve. It's in serving that DNA that you find your purpose. There is no true fulfillment in serving yourself its only in serving others. Material things and self-service will never bring you true happiness because they are temporary. The pleasure of getting something new wears off quickly. You can collect all the material things you want in life, and you will find that when the storms of life come your way. The stuff you have collected doesn't matter because it cannot truly help you or others. Accumulating stuff will never bring you the joy that helping someone else will. When you begin serving your DNA, it will give you a high like no high on this earth. I can tell you from personal experience there is no greater feeling in knowing that you helped someone out of their pit.

The meaning to your life will be found in serving your DNA.

You were not just given DNA to make your life better. You were born with it because it's to be shared. The day you discover your DNA and serve it to the world is the day you discover your purpose. It's the day you find meaning; it's the day you find your why for existing. Your meaning is tied to your DNA and your purpose is to serve that DNA. The world is waiting for you. Just imagine if Steve Jobs did not share his DNA with us. There would be no iPhone or iPad. What if Elon Musk did not share his DNA for improving the world? There would be no Tesla or Space X. What if Phil knight never shared his DNA for quality athletic shoes? There would be no Nike. Everything that you will use today comes from someone deciding to share their DNA. What DNA are you refusing to share that everyone can benefit from? What abilities are you hiding that the world could use? The success you seek is waiting for you, but it will only be found in serving your DNA.

Monica Yunus

When operating in your DNA, it will bring you to levels you never thought was possible, but those levels are not to be a service to you, but to the generation, you were born to serve. This was the case for Monica Yunus. Born in Bangladesh, she found her way to the United States at four months old after her mother and father ended their marriage. Yunus's mother decided that Bangladesh was not a place to raise a child, so she took Yunus to New Jersey and moved in with her parents. At a very young age, Yunus grandmother noticed that she had a gifted voice. Yunus's grandmother became very influential in helping her to develop her DNA by placing her in a church choir. By doing this Yunus grandmother helped her to become self-aware of her design and love for music. Though-out Yunus childhood her mother and grandmother helped her to hone in on her design which led her to become a well-known name in the opera world by the age of 15. She continued to develop her DNA by enrolling into Juilliard majoring in Vocal Performance.

After graduating Yunus secured spots in several professional operas. Her career in music became a success. While operating in the success of her design she looked for a way to contribute to her generation. In 2004, she got that opportunity. She co-founded and is the director of Sing For Hope — a nonprofit organization based in New York that brings arts programming to underprivileged communities. Yunus is now using her DNA to make a difference. Her DNA bought her success and influence. She uses that success and influence to contribute to her generation by helping others to develop their singing DNA.

Selfish people don't like sharing

Your DNA is a service that you were born with. That service was given to you to share. It is in the sharing of your DNA that creates a new world for you. What do you have to share? Selfish people can never truly understand purpose because their only desire is self-assurance. They care about no one above themselves that's why they will never be fulfilled. They will always feel a void in their life. They will never find meaning because all they care about is their success and well-being. Zig Ziegler said, "if you help enough people get what they want you will always have what you want."

Notice if you help others get what they want you will always find the success you want. I was reading the Huffington post one day and came across a compelling story about a person sharing their DNA...

The story was shared by Arianna Huffington in her book, Thrive. It was a story about her sister, Agappi, who graduated from the Royal Academy of Dramatic Art in London. Despite the success she saw and the awards she received, she was hit with a devastating blow when she didn't get a part she auditioned for in a theatre play. This causes her to second guess her design. Leaving the audition that discouraged her. She met a stranger on the public city bus where they begin to converse about theatre plays randomly. This caused Agappi to open up about the experience she just had. One thing led to another and Agappi started to do a short monologue for the woman she had just met. That monologue affected the women in a way that caused her to break out in tears because she was so moved by the acting of Agappi. At this moment Agappi felt no longer discouraged but encouraged by her DNA to perform. It was on that bus that she had learned a valuable lesson: In her words, she stated "That moment of sharing without an agenda of getting a part wasn't about the outcome but about the joy of touching others and giving unconditionally what was mine to give. And that brought with it a tremendous sense of fulfillment."

You never work being yourself.

If you honestly pay attention to the successful people around you, you will find that they have one thing in common: they provide a service to others. Serving your DNA is the thing that will bring you opportunities far beyond your imagination. Serving your DNA is responsible for the success you see in life. People who discover and serve their DNA are more efficient in their performance and live a higher quality life because serving your natural abilities gives you the opportunity to remain yourself. Being yourself causes you to stress less, and it increases your positive emotions, and it adds more get-up-and-go to your day. There is no greater feeling than being yourself. You never work serving yourself to others.

Serving your gift will open doors.

Serving your DNA will cause people with influence to find you. The DNA you were born to serve will attract money. Your DNA with proper development and use will create for you richness beyond your imagination in all aspects of your life. When you serve the DNA, you were born with doors and windows will begin to open far and wide for you. Whatever you put into your DNA is what life will give back to. Your DNA is waiting to provide you with a remarkable life. Your DNA is an investment. If you don't capitalize on it, it will never grow. You will lose the compounding interest where you and others can benefit from.

Never change the path your DNA creates for you.

There was a gentleman born by the name of Paul Terasaki. Paul's life did not start out promising for him. He was born to Japanese immigrants during World War 2. Doing the war, he and his family were forced into the internment program that relocated people of his descent to camps which deprived them of living the American dream. Living in Chicago until he graduated high school this allowed enough time to pass, so he and his family were able to move back to California after the war. This is where Terasaki enrolled into UCLA to study zoology.

While earning his master's degree, he wrote a thesis that familiarized him with transplantation science. It was the discovery of transplantation science that ignited his gift. During his postdoctoral in the UK college in London working for the predecessor of transplantation biology Sir Peter Medawar. Working with Medawar stirred Terasaki design for science. After spending one year in London, Terasaki returned to UCLA in 1956 and joined the department of surgery as an assistant research zoologist. This led him to a deep interest in cellular and molecular basis of tissue rejection. This interest steered Terasaki into creating and developing what became known as the Micro-cytotoxicity assay. This allowed doctors and the like to determine the hematology quickly or we call HLA types of both recipient and donor. This coincided with the first stirrings of what was to be the discovery of the HLA system. HLA typing had already existed in those days, but the techniques used were very unreliable and tedious. So, a Professor from Oxford's Weatherall Institute of Molecular Medicine was working at Stanford University in California where he discovered Terasaki's microcytotoxicity assay in the mid to late 1960's. After this, the test soon became the international standard test because it only required small amounts of material. Terasaki who had no qualification in medicine created a registry that collected all of the data on all of the transplants which eventually led to the system we have today of organ sharing priorities and the like. The Terasaski Testing system was born out of his design, and that design made him a very wealthy man. Using the proceeds which came from his design he put it right back into research creating the Terasaki Family foundation supporting the Terasaski Research Institute devoted to cancer immunotherapy and the study of immunity and transplantation. It was Terasaki design that saved many lives in the 1970's. The discovery of his design allowed people to find like organ donors promptly so that their life could be saved from a transplant. Terasaki was never looking for money, as a matter of fact, they had to force him to start a business because all he wanted to do was serve his design. Wealth found him when he began serving his design to others.

The pleasure is in serving.

When I discovered my DNA, I realized that for me to serve that DNA would be to teach others how to identify their DNA. My DNA is to help people find their DNA otherwise there would be no reason for the creation of this book. This book you are reading is me sharing my DNA with you. I wrote this book not for money even though money shows up in the process. I wrote this book to help you discover the unique set of DNA you were given. Nothing brings me more pleasure knowing that this book will help transform lives. So, when you get me, you get a teacher and a speaker who was designed to help others find their DNA and discover themselves. My passion lies in helping people to discover their true self who they are designed to become. Nothing makes me angrier than seeing someone waste the DNA they were born with. It twists me in such a way that I can't explain. That's because I'm passionate about people's DNA. I have invested in the lives of so many individual's DNA that it has crippled my family and me at times. My wife had to put brakes on me because I love to see people operating in their DNA that I would at time invest all the money we had into them, not knowing that people would take advantage of your resources. Those experiences taught me a lot about myself. It helped me to recognize people who wanted to discover themselves and the ones who did not. Now I can recognize where to invest my resources, and that's into people like you, or you would not be reading this book. I offer DNA consulting for 30 minutes so if you are unsure or have questions concerning your DNA, please contact our office by going to www.donnielnelson.com because we want nothing more than for you to become who your DNA designed you to be. My life assignment and purpose are to help you discover the DNA you were born with, and I will do whatever it takes within my power to do so. What purpose do you serve in the lives of others? When you go away, what goes with you? You were born to solve a problem. I'm a gift influencer. I help people to find who they were designed to become. I was designed to help you solve the question, about success in life? I was born to bring things that are hidden on the inside of you to the light so that you can discover who you are. I'm the response to people not understanding their DNA. I'm the response to untapped potential. I'm the response to self- discovery. The reason many individuals don't succeed is because they fail to become the responds to the problem they were built to solve. The success in every individual start with them discovering the void they are to fulfill in the lives of other individuals.

What problem where you born to respond to? Joe Gebbia was created with the DNA to solve the problem of unaffordable lodging during travel or everyday living. He has made it possible for 260 million people in 65000 cities to find affordable lodging. Joe Gebbia is the Co-Founder of Airbnb which is a person to person home and apartment rental company. His services to others have created for him a net worth of $3.3 billion according to Forbes. Jack Ma was created with the DNA to solve the problem of small business exportation. Small businesses in China had no way of selling and exporting products they produced to other markets, so Jack Ma created Alibaba to solve that problem. Many small businesses in China have become very successful today because of Jack Ma. His contribution to his country has made him worth $40.3 billion according to Forbes. When you discover your DNA and begin serving it, you will find that it deploys you. It's in serving your DNA that you will find your business. There is a reason for you being born where you were born, to the parents you were born to and even the journey that you have been through thus far. You were prepared for this particular generation and assigned to contribute something specific to it?

Your DNA makes you Influential.

Every person on this planet was born with a specific set of DNA. A set of DNA that is uniquely his or hers. No one has the same set of DNA although everyone has DNA. Your DNA is unique to you. It's your natural resource, you have to dig to discover it, and once you discover it, you have to remove the dust and polish your DNA so that you can use it to become an influence on your generation. Your DNA gives you the power to influence others in a way that will affect action and change within them. It gives you the ability to capture the hearts and minds of people. Your DNA is constructed to make you influential once you discover and serve it. You were born with influence. Your DNA is that influence. When you find who your DNA designed you to serve, you find your influence. My DNA designed me to help people discover their unique set of DNA. Therefore, my influence is helping people discover their abilities and what their DNA designed them to become. Who has your DNA designed you to serve? Nelson Mandela, Martin Luther King Jr., and Mahatma Gandhi DNA designed him to serve those who suffered injustice. Walt Disney DNA designed him to serve kids by creating a world of entertainment specially made for kids. Sam

Walton DNA designed him to serve local communities by creating jobs and saving people money by selling more for less. The Wright brothers' DNA designed them to serve in global transportation by helping people get to places faster in a shorter amount of time. Clara Barton DNA designed her to serve those in need during disasters and catastrophic times. She is the founder of the American Red Cross, a humanitarian organization that provides emergency assistance, disaster relief and education in the United States. Sara Blakely DNA designed her to serve the body of women. She created a product called Spanx that helped shape the trouble areas of women's bodies to give them a flawless figure look. If you were to follow the lives of every individual I have just named, then you will notice that their influence came by the way of their DNA. Influence was not given to them by the things they created or by the education they received or by their fame. Their influence came only because of them willing to find a way to serve their DNA to mankind. Neither of these men or women sought to become influential they were just focused on refining and serving their unique set of DNA that they became influential being themselves. You do not need to become anyone else but yourself to make an impact on the world. You just have to discover what your DNA designed you to be and allow that design to be a service to your generation. You will know when you are serving your DNA in the area you were designed for when people start looking for you in that area. My wife has a gift for beauty so when people want something done or have a question concerning beauty they find her because beauty is a part of her DNA. So, therefore, the influence that she holds is in those areas. When you serve your DNA in the area you were designed to serve in you will discover your significance to your generation and that significance brings influence, and that influence comes because of the value your DNA creates. That's why this book was created because everyone on earth has inherent DNA to become something great, but who and what they are is an individual discovery and I hope reading this book has brought you a step closer to the discovery of yourself. Once you find and refine your DNA, it will create for you a life that you have not imagine.

Make a promise to yourself that you'll dig to find your natural resource, so that the world may benefit. Make it a personal mandate to discover the DNA you were born with.

NOTES

Chapter 1

Jack Ma
The Inc website
https://www.inc.com/business-insider/alibaba-jack-ma-life-story.html
https://www.cbsnews.com/news/alibaba-chairman-jack-ma-brings-company-to-america/
Page 17-22

Vera Wang
Business of Fashion Website
Page 32-34

Chapter 2

Jay Z
The Biography Website
https://www.biography.com/musician/jay-z
Page 37-41

NOTES

Chapter 3

Mother Teresa
https://www.biography.com/people/mother-teresa- 9504160
Page 52-54

Wendy Kopp
http://www.achievement.org/achiever/wendy-kopp/
Page 57

National Public radio interview
page 58-60

J.K Rowling
https://www.biography.com/people/jk-rowling-40998
Page 61-62

Chapter 4

Webster definition
Page 74

NOTES

Chapter 6

Psychologists Ulrich Weger and Stephen
Loughnan
https://www.scientificamerican.com/article/yo
ur-thoughts-can- release-abilities-beyond-
normal-limits/
Page 135-136

Chapter 7

Warren Buffett
https://www.biography.com/people/warren-
buffett- 920729
Page 145-147

Phil Knight
https://www.entrepreneur.com/article/197534
Page 155-157

NOTES

Chapter 8

Stanford New webstie
https://news.stanford.edu/2005/06/14/jobs-061505/
Page 167-169

Chapter 9

Monica Yunus
https://en.wikipedia.org/wiki/Monica_Yunus
Page 180-182

Huffington Post Arianna Huffington Thrive
Page 183-184

Paul Terasaki's
http://www.onelambda.com/en/about-us/news/recent-news/terasaki-news.html
Page 186-189

Joe Gebbia Airbnb
https://www.forbes.com/profile/joe-gebbia/
Page 192